Reducing offending:

an assessment of research evidence on ways of dealing with offending behaviour

Directed by
Christopher Nuttall

Edited by
Peter Goldblatt
Chris Lewis

A Research and Statistics Directorate Report

Home Office
Research and
Statistics
Directorate

London: Home Office

Home Office Research Studies

The Home Office Research Studies are reports on research undertaken by or on behalf of the Home Office. They cover the range of subjects for which the Home Secretary has responsibility. Titles in the series are listed at the back of this report (copies are available from the address on the back cover). Other publications produced by the Research and Statistics Directorate include Research Findings, the Research Bulletin, Statistical Bulletins and Statistical Papers.

The Research and Statistics Directorate

The Directorate consists of three Units which deal with research and statistics on Crime and Criminal Justice, Offenders and Corrections, Immigration and General Matters; the Programme Development Unit; the Economics Unit; and the Operational Research Unit.

The Research and Statistics Directorate is an integral part of the Home Office, serving the Ministers and the department itself, its services, Parliament and the public through research, development and statistics. Information and knowledge from these sources informs policy development and the management of programmes; their dissemination improves wider public understanding of matters of Home Office concern.

First published 1998

Application for reproduction should be made to the Information and Publications Group, Room 201, Home Office, 50 Queen Anne's Gate, London SW1H 9AT.

Acknowledgements

This report is the result of the work of many people. I chaired a two-day workshop at which authors of chapters in this report presented their material. In each case the issues raised were then discussed, initiated by an invited lead discussant. Patrticipants were:

Authors:	John Graham	Home Office
	Paul Ekblom	Home Office
	Ken Pease	University of Huddersfield
	Tim Hope	University of Keele
	Peter Jordan	Home Office
	David Moxon	Home Office
	Julie Vennard	Home Office
	Peter Goldblatt	Home Office
Lead discussants:	David Farrington	University of Cambridge
	Hugh Marriage	Home Office
	James McGuire	University of Liverpool
	Lawrence Sherman	University of Maryland
	Jan van Dijk	Ministry of Justice, The Netherlands
	Irvin Waller	International Centre for the Prevention of Crime, Montreal
	Norman Warner	Home Office
	Brandon Welsh	International Centre for the Prevention of Crime, Montreal
Other participants:	John Ditchfield	Home Office
	Marian FitzGerald	Home Office
	Gloria Laycock	Home Office
	Chris Lewis	Home Office
	Jerry Lee	B-101, Philadelphia
	Liz Lloyd	Prime Minister's Office
	John Lyon	Home Office
	Pat Mayhew	Home Office
	Richard Price	HM Treasury

I am absolutely delighted by the result. The final work of summarising the chapters into a manageable and, I think, useful report was done by Peter

Goldblatt and Chris Lewis. I am extremely grateful to them and to Michelle Washer, who organised the seminar at Heathrow, for the timeliness, flexibility, creativity and professionalism of the enterprise.

CHRISTOPHER NUTTALL

Director
Research and Statistics
Home Office

Contents

Executive summary

The aim of this report is to assess, from the available research evidence, the comparative effectiveness and cost-effectiveness of different methods of reducing crime. On the basis of this evidence, options for inclusion in an integrated and evolving portfolio of interventions are identified.

To this end, the report summarises evidence on:

- **promoting a less criminal society** by preventing the development of criminality among young people and investing in situational crime prevention to reduce the opportunities for crime;

- **preventing crime in the community** by acting on the social conditions that sustain crime in residential communities and by implementing effective police strategies for reducing crime; and,

- **criminal justice interventions** through changes in sentencing policy or extending the use of effective interventions with offenders and drug users.

In addressing these issues the questions considered are

- how effective is the intervention (and can the benefits be quantified)?;

- what evidence is available on the likely costs of implementation?;

- what is the likely timescale for the costs and benefits?;

- how strong is the available evidence on effects, costs and timescales?;

- how likely is it that the results quoted in the research will translate into effective implementation?;

- how extensive are the programmes that could be implemented on the basis of current research evidence?; and,

- what organisational or institutional arrangements are suggested by the research for effectively implementing strategies for crime reduction?

Despite significant gaps in our knowledge on each of these points, a number of conclusions emerge.

(i)   The criminal justice system has a central role in providing the sanctions to enforce or reinforce compliance with the law, on which other crime reduction initiatives depend.

(ii)   Efforts to redirect funds to more effective crime reduction tools, within or outside this system, will have only a gradual impact in reducing crime. However, if the reductions claimed by the most promising approaches are realised, the long term reductions in crime that would be achieved are substantial. Only by large-scale piloting of these approaches can a judgement be reached on their operational effectiveness.

(iii)   None of the initiatives identified as promising will reduce crime on its own. An effective crime reduction strategy is one in which an integrated package of best practice is developed and delivered consistently over time.

(iv)   The components of an effective and integrated strategy would draw on:

- intensive interventions among children and families at risk;

- increasing informal social control and social cohesion in communities and institutions that are vulnerable to crime, criminality, drug usage and disorder;

- intervention in the development of products or services vulnerable to crime so as to make them less so;

- incentives to individuals and organisations to reduce the risk of crime;

- targeting situational prevention measures on "hot spots" and areas of high risk generally;

- reducing repeat victimisation;

- placing greater emphasis on problem oriented policing;

- extending the range of effective interventions with offenders and drug users;

- making more use, in appropriate circumstances, of penalties such as fines and curfew orders with tagging; and,

- improving the consistency of sentencing.

(v)   Any portfolio should combine long term investment in children and families with actions that would yield more immediate, though probably smaller returns (such as situational prevention). It would also include activities aimed at achieving gains that accumulate steadily (such as offender programmes, community action and improved product design). There is evidence that such an approach would be cost-effective throughout its life, with substantial cost benefits in the long run.

1 Introduction

This report was commissioned by a working group of the Cross Departmental Review of the Criminal Justice System (CJS) on the effectiveness of dealing with offending behaviour. The review was part of the Comprehensive Spending Review (CSR), launched when the current Government took office in May 1997 to "reshape the pattern of public expenditure now and into the next century" so as to match their priorities.

The work, on which the report is based, had in fact started about two years earlier and was initially taken forward by Simon Field of the Research and Statistics Directorate at the Home Office. It had become increasingly clear that research evidence produced over the previous 40-50 years indicated that certain approaches to reducing crime would be more effective than others. It was not true that "nothing works". The aim, in putting together this report, was to summarise the evidence that "some things work under some conditions" and to assess to what extent this evidence was "generalizable to similar settings in other places and times" (Sherman et al., 1997). By doing this we hoped to identify a set of "what works" principles, at the broadest level, that would provide the basis for a crime reduction strategy. As the CSR was intended to shift resources to where they will do most to achieve the Government's objectives, this assessment was needed to indicate what would constitute the most cost-effective strategy to reverse a long-term trend, which has seen recorded crime increase by about 5 per cent per year since the 1920s (Figure 1.1).

The approach taken was to commission substantive contributions on the main approaches to containing or reducing crime from experts in each field. A wider group of experts, administrators and political advisors then attended a two-day seminar to discuss these contributions. The original material was amended by the authors to take account of comments and then summarised for inclusion in this report.

In producing this assessment of the evidence, several recent reviews were particularly influential. In 1996 the US Congress required the Attorney General to provide a comprehensive evaluation of the effectiveness of the Department of Justice's grants to assist in the prevention of crime. An independent review of the scientific literature was commissioned for that evaluation. The report on that work (Sherman et al., 1997) has informed this

Figure 1.1   Recorded Crime, 1918-1997
(logarithmic scale)

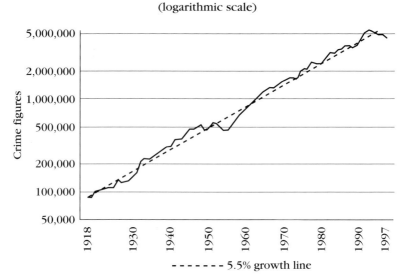

-------- 5.5% growth line

study. In particular, one feature of their analysis was to employ a scientific methods scale to rate the "methodological rigor" of the studies quoted in evidence (see Annex A). This scale (and the associated classification of "what works") are used descriptively in several chapters of this report. However they have not formed the sole basis for judging effectiveness or strength of evidence here.

A "Crime Prevention Digest", prepared by the International Centre for the Prevention of Crime (1997), summarised the substantial reductions in crime achieved by various interventions in a number of countries and compared their cost-effectiveness. Material from this Digest (and subsequent papers by Brandon Welsh, the co-ordinator of the work) have been adapted in this report to compare the cost-benefit ratios associated with different interventions. Significant use was also made of a critical account of the effectiveness of a range of crime reduction strategies and measures in Europe and North America, prepared for the United Nations (Graham and Bennett, 1995).

The individual chapters in this report cover a variety of techniques to reduce the frequency, seriousness or cost of crime or disorder. Criminal events (or disorder) occur when individuals with a propensity to engage in criminal or disorderly behaviour are in situations which encourage or facilitate this type of behaviour. The report first presents evidence on how to reduce the number of children and young people who develop this propensity, how to intervene in the opportunities for crime and how to build reduced vulnerability to crime into new products, environments and policies.

Prevention in the community, through community crime prevention and better policing, is then examined. Finally, the evidence that interventions with existing offenders might deter, incapacitate or rehabilitate is reviewed.

The findings are summarised in Chapter 9 and it is concluded that this evidence provides the basis for a coherent and co-ordinated strategy which recognises that:

- none of the initiatives identified as promising will control crime on its own. An effective crime reduction strategy is one in which an integrated package of best practice is developed and delivered consistently over time;

- multiple interventions are generally more cost-effective than initiatives with a single focus. For example, prevention programmes for young people should target risk factors affecting all aspects of a child's life;

- advantage should be taken of evidence which identifies particular initiatives which would have an early but not necessarily lasting effect on offending behaviour and therefore the crime rate;

- many promising initiatives bring their main crime reduction benefits over a long period. However they have earlier, beneficial effects on other outcomes (education, employment, informal social control and family cohesion), the absence of which are predictors of subsequent criminality. The effect on these risk factors therefore needs to be carefully monitored, evaluated and reviewed to ensure the full potential of the initiatives is realised (and ineffectual interventions stopped);

- implementation of initiatives more generally should be planned so as to ensure that the ìwhat worksî principles are adhered to and adequate and appropriate training and evaluation are included. The evidence that emerges from evaluation should be used to inform the running and performance monitoring of the main Government programmes to which they relate; and,

- evidence on effectiveness, and more particularly cost effectiveness, is currently limited, cannot easily be extrapolated nationally from small-scale pilots and is not collected in a way which allows for comparisons between initiatives. Process and impact evaluation should therefore be designed to generate both cost and effectiveness information.

References

International Centre for the Prevention of Crime (1997). *'Crime Prevention Digest.'* Montreal.

Graham, J. and Bennett, T. (1995). *'Crime Prevention Strategies in Europe and North America.'* HEUNI: Helsinki.

Sherman, L. W. et al. (1997). *'Preventing Crime: What works, what doesn't, what's promising.'* Office of Justice Programs Research Report, U.S. Department of Justice: Washington DC.

Section I

Promoting a less criminal society

2 What works in preventing criminality

John Graham

Introduction

This chapter deals with preventing criminality by reducing the number of children and young people with a disposition to behave persistently in a criminal manner. It gives examples of cost-effective delivery of criminality prevention initiatives.

Targeting known risk factors

We know a good deal about the risk factors which can result in criminal behaviour. They include: poverty and poor housing; poor parenting (including neglect, abuse, harsh and inconsistent discipline, lack of supervision and marital conflict); association with delinquent peers, siblings and partners; low measures of intelligence, poor school performance and persistent truancy; high levels of impulsiveness and hyperactivity; and being brought up by a criminal parent or parents (Farrington, 1996).

Although we cannot predict accurately which individual will become an offender on the basis of the level of risk to which they are exposed, we know that children exposed to multiple risks are disproportionately likely to end up as serious or persistent offenders (Graham and Bowling, 1995). Also, those who engage in anti-social or criminal behaviour at an early age are more likely to become serious and persistent offenders (Home Office, 1987).

These risk factors are generally part of a pattern of childhood anti-social behaviour (Capaldi and Patterson, 1996) and differ little from risk factors associated with other youthful deviant behaviour (Dryfoos, 1990; Hawkins and Catalano, 1992). Thus, programmes to prevent criminality can be part of wider programmes to address a range of problematic outcomes for young people, such as substance abuse, school failure and teenage pregnancy. In theory at least, such programmes can be highly cost-effective since the return on any given investment will extend well beyond reductions in criminality

What works?

To establish what works in preventing criminality, we must be confident that initiatives have been well evaluated. Many evaluations are weak in design and very few meet the highest standards of scientific rigour. This chapter follows the classification used in the review for the US Congress (Sherman et al., 1997) and described in more detail in Annex A. Only those evaluations where the strength of the evidence is such that they would be classified in the top two grades of the five-level classification are included in the assessment presented here.

In this chapter we classify initiatives in criminality prevention into those which are family-based, those which are school-based and those which are peer group-based.

Family-based initiatives

Family-based interventions can be divided into three main types: early home visits and pre-school education programmes; family therapy and parent training; and family preservation.

i)   Early home visits and pre-school education programmes

Sherman (1997) indicates that the most promising results in preventing crime are to be found in home visitation programmes. These involve trained and committed individuals, usually nurses, health visitors or social workers, supporting, helping and sometimes training parents of young children. Such programmes have consistently shown positive effects on crime or crime risk factors. Sherman (1997) summarised the findings from 18 such evaluations. The two most important – *the Syracuse Family Development Programme* and the *Perry Pre-School Programme* – measure the long term impact of home visitation on delinquency.

The *Syracuse Family Development Programme* provided pre and post natal advice and support to low income, predominantly African-American women. Whereas 22 per cent of the control group had been convicted for criminal offences by age 15, only six per cent of the experimental group had convictions and these tended to be for less serious offences (Lally et al., 1988).

The *High/Scope Perry Pre-School Programme* targeted both children and their parents. A total of 58 black children from low socio-economic families received a two year high quality pre-school education programme in the early 1960s, whilst their mothers received home visits. The subsequent fortunes of the children were contrasted with a matched control group.

Those who attended the programme performed better in school and adult education, were more likely to graduate and get employment and were about half as likely to be pregnant during their teens. Arrest rates were 40 per cent lower for the experimental group at age 19 (Figure 2.1). By age 27, the children who had attended pre-school were significantly more likely to have completed their education and be earning more than $2,000 a month (Figure 2.2). In the control group 35 per cent had been arrested five or more times, compared with seven per cent of those who had attended the pre-school programme (Schweinhart and Weikart, 1993). A cost benefit analysis based on these figures indicated a return of $7 for every $1 invested (see Table 2.1).

Figure 2.1 *High/Scope Perry Preschool Study: Effects of the programme at age 19*

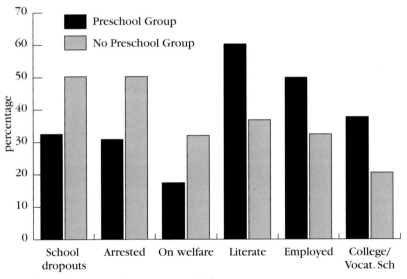

Source: J.R. Berrueta-Clement et. al. (1984)

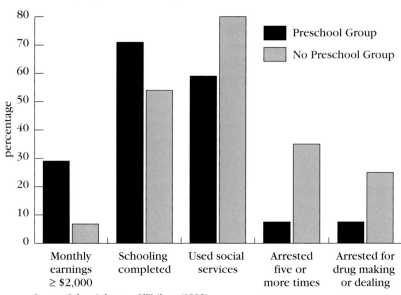

Figure 2.2   High/Scope Perry Preschool Study: Effects of the programme at age 27

Source: Schweinhart and Weikart (1993)

These findings are remarkable, given the time between the intervention and the outcomes. However, the samples are small and the target group highly specific in terms of its socio-economic background. Similar experiments with larger samples of individuals and families from a wider range of target groups need to be undertaken. It should be noted, however, that Weikart (co-founder of the project) has indicated that the multiple benefits of the Perry pre-school project have led insurance companies to fund similar programmes on the basis of their long term return on investment (i.e. they are more likely to do well at school, find long term stable employment and therefore purchase a house and a car).

Ten of the other evaluations reviewed by Sherman (1997) focus on crime risk factors and measure outcomes in terms of later reductions in anti-social behaviour and improvements in children's cognitive skills, parental attachment and parenting skills: a further five were evaluated in terms of their impact on child abuse. All show positive outcomes.

Such programmes often have large effects for both parents and children, especially those at high risk. The Rochester University study, for example, achieved a 79 per cent relative reduction in child abuse for high risk mothers. Similarly, the Syracuse Family Development Programme achieved a 73 per cent reduction in probation referrals by age 15 (Lally et al., 1988) and in a 15-year follow up of the Elmira Program in New York, Olds et al.

(1997) reported 69 per cent fewer arrests, 44 per cent fewer substance abuse related behavioural problems experienced by the mothers and 46 per cent fewer reports of child abuse in the experimental group. Most recently, Karoly et al. (1998) from the RAND Corporation assessed the cost-benefits of nine programmes which were accompanied by high quality evaluations and concluded that the size of the effects were mostly substantial.

Whilst large effect sizes may be the exception rather than the rule (Sherman, 1997), positive effects clearly do endure and could lead to substantial reductions in serious crime in the future. Sherman (1997) estimated that, on the basis of the evidence on reductions in child abuse alone, a universal US home visitation programme, for example, would prevent half a million serious crimes. If a similar proportion of parental neglect cases were also prevented, there could be a further 800,000 fewer serious crimes committed in later life by the children.

ii)   Family therapy and parent training

Sherman (1997) reviewed 17 family therapy and parent training programmes. Three programmes which measured their impact on delinquency showed moderately positive effects. One programme, which provided training for parents of 10-year-old children for a period of six to eight months, showed reductions in self-reported delinquency after one year (Kazdin et al. 1992). In another, training of parents and social skills training for 160 seven-year-old boys over two years produced a similar reduction in self-reported offending after six years and a small reduction in officially recorded delinquency (Tremblay et al., 1995). A third programme providing 1,600 children aged six, their parents and their teachers with skills training over a four-year period showed a short term reduction in self-reported delinquency and improvements in parenting and attachment to family and school (Hawkins et al., 1992).

Of the other 11 programmes, four were based in clinics and targeted the parents of children aged between 7 and 12 and seven were home based involving parents of children between the ages of three and five. All programmes delivered various forms of parent training, counselling and therapy and in some cases children were also the subjects of behavioural interventions. With one qualified exception (Dishion et al., 1992), all the evaluations showed reductions in anti-social behaviour, conduct disorders and/or improvements in parenting.

There are few similar programmes in the UK but work is being undertaken at Maudsley Hospital in London with severely aggressive children and their families. This uses video-tapes and one-way mirrors to show parents how to control the behaviour of their children without resorting to physical punishments or threats. Unpublished findings from a pilot study suggest that improvements in children's behaviour are sustained for two years beyond the 10 to 12 week course (Utting, 1996).

Overall, parent training courses do seem to be able to help parents respond more constructively, use discipline less harshly and more consistently and avoid situations which precipitate conflict. The most promising approaches combine parent training with other strategies, such as social and problem solving skills for the parent's children (Kazdin et al., 1992) and pro-active classroom management and peer-related strategies for older children (O'Donnell et al., 1995).

iii)   Family preservation

Family preservation comprises intensive interventions with families where parent:child relationships are under severe stress or breaking down and the child is at risk of being taken into care. Given the considerable potential savings of avoiding out-of-home placements, family preservation programmes are likely to be cost-effective if they also reduce later crime and delinquency. The available evidence on effectiveness is limited, although family preservation projects in the states of Washington (Tacoma Homebuilders) and Michigan (Families First) have shown success in terms of keeping children out of care (Utting et al., 1993). According to Utting et al. (1993), projects which report success in working with such families tend to be those which emphasise the need to raise parental self-esteem and build on the existing strengths of the parents concerned.

A comprehensive strategy of early intervention would consist of providing an integrated package of pre-school education for the child and support and training for the child's parents, including intensive therapy in extreme cases. But whilst early interventions show much promise and are necessary for effective prevention in the early years, they need to be supplemented with other strategies. As the child begins to explore the outside world, the importance of family life and parenting recede as school and peer group influences increase.

School-based initiatives

School-based interventions aim to reduce the propensity to engage in delinquent and anti-social behaviour. They can be divided into projects which aim to influence the organisation and ethos of schools; anti-bullying initiatives and family:school partnerships.

i) Organisational change programmes

In the early 1980s, the US Office of Juvenile Justice and Delinquency Prevention funded 17 diverse, school-based, delinquency prevention programmes in high crime areas under their Alternative Education Initiative. The initiative was based on the premise that by altering the organisation of schools, delinquency and associated problems of dropout, disruptive behaviour and truancy could be prevented. Various strategies were tested, ranging from peer counselling to school climate improvement. Overall, some positive findings were recorded, including greater safety, less teacher victimisation, small falls in delinquency, decreases in alienation and improvements in pupil self-concept.

The *PATHE project* combined institutional change with individually-based initiatives to increase educational attainment and reduce delinquent behaviour in four high and four middle schools in predominantly black, inner city areas (Gottfredson and Gottfredson, 1986). The results show that those elements of the projects concerned with *institutional change* had a small but measurable effect on delinquency and school conduct one year after the programme was implemented. The most dramatic improvement occurred in pupils' reports and official recordings of suspensions in the three experimental high schools, which dropped by 14 per cent on average. In the control high school, the suspension rate **increased** by 10per cent. However, similar improvements were not recorded for academic performance, attendance and self-concept, although there were improvements in attachment to school and significant decreases in school alienation.

In contrast, the initiatives based on *individuals* had no effect on delinquency, attachment to school or pupil self-concepts, but did improve the commitment of at risk pupils to education as indicated by small improvements in attendance and academic performance.

A second evaluation of a similar initiative – the *Effective Schools Project* – reported considerably larger reductions in delinquency after two years (Gottfredson, 1987). This project introduced measures to improve the clarity of rules and the consistency with which they are enforced; co-operative learning; frequent monitoring of students' work; expansion of extracurricular activities; and improved career-related motivation and participation.

On the whole, research on school effectiveness shows that schools which are characterised by high quality classroom management, good leadership and organisation and where children feel emotionally as well as educationally supported, are those which are best placed to protect their pupils from engaging in criminal behaviour.

ii)   Anti-bullying initiatives

School bullies are particularly at risk of becoming serious violent offenders and are also more likely to raise children who become bullies themselves (Farrington, 1993). In Bergen, Norway a "whole school" approach to combat bullying has been implemented in 42 schools. The initiative introduced specific rules about bullying, the insertion of discussions on bullying into the curriculum, encouragement to victims to report incidents of bullying and better systems of playground supervision. In addition to marked reductions in bullying, the initiative resulted in reductions in anti-social behaviour and victimisation outside school. The positive effects endured for at least 20 months (Olweus, 1990 and 1991).

In England, a similar "whole school" anti-bullying approach in 23 schools in Sheffield included setting out precise procedures for preventing and responding to bullying, improving playground supervision and implementing courses for improving problem-solving skills and assertiveness. The programme was successful in reducing bullying in primary schools, but had relatively small effects in secondary schools (Smith and Sharp, 1994).

Another anti-bullying initiative within a violence prevention project in two high crime public housing estates in East London and Merseyside targeted two primary and two secondary schools. As in Bergen and Sheffield, a "whole school" approach was adopted: improvements in the supervision and surveillance of play areas during breaks, confidential contacts for victims and discussion groups for parents were introduced. Two years later, levels of bullying had decreased in three of the schools (Pitts and Smith, 1995).

iii)   Family/school partnerships

To be effective, early intervention needs to improve both the parenting and the education of children at risk, preferably sustained throughout childhood. The best way to accomplish this is to forge partnerships between the two principal sources of socialisation and informal social control – families and schools (Graham and Utting, 1996). A few projects in the US have begun to adopt this approach.

In Oregon, a universal intervention programme to prevent conduct disorders has been developed (Reid et al., 1994). *LIFT (Linking Interests of Families and Teachers)* focuses on encouraging pro-social and discouraging anti-social behaviour at home and at school through parent training, social skills classes for the children, playground behaviour strategies and the installation of a school-to-home telephone line. Initial findings suggest an immediate impact in terms of reducing aggressive and anti-social behaviour.

The *FAST Track programme* is potentially one of the most promising family:school initiatives (Conduct Problems Prevention Research Group, 1992). It builds upon the links which develop between parents and schools during the early years by developing strategies to sustain and improve these links. The main goals are to reduce anti-social behaviour in the home/school by improving parent/child and family/school relationships and the child's academic, social and cognitive development. The main mechanisms for achieving these goals are parent training, bi-weekly home visits, social skills training, academic tutoring and teacher-based classroom interventions to improve behavioural management.

To encourage parents to help their children succeed in school, they are shown how to set up a structured learning environment to encourage their learning and how to communicate with the school and develop a positive relationship with the child's teacher. Simultaneously, parents are shown through home visits how to help their children implement anger control and problem-solving strategies taught to the children in the classroom. Family co-ordinators are used to help parents to solve some of their own problems. They are allocated to families for several years, so they have enough time to build up trust and explore interpersonal relationships within the family. Early findings suggest that after one year, the experimental groups are showing signs of improvements in cognitive skills, problem behaviour and parental involvement in the child's education (Dodge, 1993).

Peer group-based initiatives

Associating with criminal peer groups is an important factor in subsequent criminality. However influencing this is very difficult and there are very few examples of successful interventions. One exception is the South Baltimore Youth Centre project, which has built on the work of the Milton S. Eisenhower Foundation for the Prevention of Violence. The project incorporates the best elements of two other projects, El Centro and Argus, both of which are community based projects set up to tackle drug misuse and serious crime in the inner city (see Graham and Bennett, 1995). The project provides a safe environment for young people at risk to establish a life based on trust, mutual respect, and co-operation. Recruits form an extended family with youth workers who act as their mentors and advocates. Contracts are signed and peer pressure is used to exercise discipline and control. Members are taught to control their anger and confront their fears and where possible are offered job training linked to real jobs. Serious delinquent behaviour decreased by a third among those on the programme, compared to a small increase in the control group, over a period of 19 months (Baker et al., 1995).

What doesn't work?

There are many more examples of programmes which have been shown not to work than those which do. Dryfoos (1990) and Gottfredson (1997) list a number of preventive interventions which have been evaluated and found not to work. These include individual casework, individual and peer group counselling/therapy (the latter may even be counter-productive), pharmacological interventions (except for specific forms of violent offending), corporal punishment, suspension from school, information campaigns (especially in relation to substance abuse), diversion to leisure and recreation facilities, fear arousal (e.g. "scare 'em straight") and moral appeals. Many of these were based on single measure interventions and it is now accepted that, to be effective, prevention programmes need to comprise a range of complementary measures which target multiple risk factors within the primary domains of a child's life (the family, the school, the peer group and the local neighbourhood), preferably at different developmental stages (early childhood, primary school, adolescence) – Hawkins et al. (1992).

It is also recognised that to be effective, programmes should target behavioural change and not just changes in attitudes, values or knowledge. Sometimes failed programmes continue to be funded on the grounds that the evaluation was faulty (which in some cases is justified) or that the effects have not occurred yet (which may also be justifiable in some cases). It is important, however, to ensure that expenditure on interventions which have not been shown to work are curtailed and to do this it is necessary to highlight those interventions which have been shown to be ineffective in a variety of settings.

How cost-effective is criminality prevention?

Good scientific evidence on what works in preventing criminality is scarce and almost entirely restricted to a few US projects. Few evaluations provide sufficiently detailed data for a reliable assessment of cost-effectiveness. Although similar prevention programmes exist in the UK, they have not been evaluated to the same standards as in the US. None provide cost data in a form which allows an economic assessment. It is therefore not known whether the projects described below would be as successful if replicated in the UK.

Welsh (in press) has reviewed the literature on the cost-effectiveness of initiatives to prevent criminality. In all, he found nine studies in the US and Canada which provided cost data, of which only seven provided sufficient detail to allow some form of economic analysis. Subjects ranged from pre-birth to 18. Most projects targeted children in their early years and most were implemented in the home, although one, Job Corps, targeted older youths. All but two of the studies had follow-up periods of 16 months or more. Table 2.1, adapted from Welsh, summarises the available evidence.

Six of the seven studies show a favourable cost-benefit outcome. The economic return on one unit of monetary investment ranged from 1.06 units to 7.16 units. The most promising were found to be those which targeted babies, infants and pre-school children. Savings from reduced crime and delinquency accounted for a substantial proportion of the measured benefits. Other monetary benefits included less reliance on welfare payments, more subjects employed (and therefore increased tax revenues), less use of remedial education and less use of security and emergency services.

Other considerations

It is important to identify not only what works in preventing criminality, but also how carefully designed criminality prevention programmes can be successfully implemented. On the basis of the evidence to date, there are a number of principles which stand out as important components in the successful design and implementation of effective programmes. These need to be incorporated into any strategy which is evidence-based and problem oriented. An important consideration is how to find the right balance between targeting resources on those individuals and neighbourhoods most at risk where the benefits are likely to be greatest, whilst ensuring that the investment is not wasted by the need, for example, to re-establish social control in an area suffering from a breakdown of law and order.

Evidence from the US and The Netherlands suggests that a strategic approach to preventing crime and criminality needs to combine a 'top down' approach with a 'bottom up' approach which builds on existing local resources, especially informal support networks (Bright, 1997). Existing knowledge further suggests that effective interventions need to target more than one risk factor, involve the delivery of more than one service, start early (but not exclusively) and last for a relatively long time. Early interventions need to be supplemented with developmentally appropriate "booster" sessions throughout the childhood of those most at risk.

Other important components include:

• The involvement of target groups in the design and implementation of programmes;

• Sensitivity to the importance of culturally diverse norms and values;

- The employment of professional staff with training in preventive work and inter-agency collaboration; and,

- An independent, scientifically rigorous evaluation which incorporates process and outcome elements, adopts some form of experimental design if possible and measures effectiveness across a range of outcomes.

Conclusions

This chapter shows that a wide range of initiatives which target children, their families, their schools and their friends prevent criminality or reduce related risk factors. It also shows that some of these initiatives are cost-effective, with the best producing substantial returns on an initial investment. Early interventions to target not only the children at risk but also their parents and their schools are most beneficial. They deliver multiple outcomes and can be far more cost-effective than initiatives whose focus is only to prevent crime (Hawkins and Catalano, 1992).

Most of the evidence cited in this report is based on studies from North America. We cannot be sure that what works in one country will work equally well in another. The widespread ownership of firearms, the absence of a universal public health service, the ethnic minority composition of many inner city areas and a long history of widespread use of hard drugs are just some of the features of American society which are different from ours. It is important therefore that we begin to develop strategies for testing preventive interventions in our own country.

There are many promising approaches in England and Wales which have yet to be rigorously evaluated. Utting (1997) describes over 30 such approaches. It may be that some of these will prove more cost-effective than those for which fully evaluated evidence is currently available. One approach to testing their effectiveness would be to develop an initiative in a selection of appropriate small areas, concentrating resources in existing institutions, such as family centres and schools. This would provide a constructive intermediate stage between moving from project-based interventions on a small scale to the mainstreaming of policies to prevent criminality and related outcomes on a national scale. It could also be used to address issues of targeting, such as the universal allocation of resources versus focusing on neighbourhoods or families.

This investment will require a long term perspective. On the basis of results from a comparative study of US evidence conducted by the RAND Corporation, long term crime strategies that divert children from crime promise to be cost-effective (Greenwood et al., 1996; Karoly et al., 1998).

Table 2.1 Estimated cost benefits obtained in studies to prevent criminality

Project	Stage of dev.	Risk factors targeted	Length of intervention	Length of follow up	Outcomes	Cost-benefit
1.	Pre-natal	Parenting and family planning	2 years	2 years	Reductions in abuse, neglect; improvements in parent:child relations, IQ and parental discipline	1.06
2.	Pre-natal and birth	Parenting, and family planning	4 years	None	Reductions in abuse and neglect	0.38
3.	Age 3–4	Cognitive develpment	1–2 years	23 years	Reductions in arrests and contact with social services; improvements in IQ and school achievement	7.16
4.	Age 5–15	Family environment	32 months	16 months	Reductions in arrests; improvements in self-concept, pro-social skills and community integration	2.55
5.	Age 15 (av.)	Education	4 years	6 months	Reductions in arrests and contacts with social services; improvements in school achiev.	3.68
6.	Age under 15 (av.)	Delinquency and behavioural problems	10 weeks	None	Reductions in arrests	1.40
7.	Age 18 (av.)	Education, unemployment	Not avail.	18 months (average)	Reductions in arrests and substance abuse; improvements in employment, wages and school achievement	1.45

Key to projects:
1. = Elmira Nurse Home Visitation; 2 = Hawaii Healthy Start; 3 = Perry High/Scope Pre-school; 4 = Participate and Learn Skills (PALS); 5 = Quantum Opportunities; 6 = Los Angeles County Delinquency Prevention; 7 = Job Corps.

Source: Adapted from Welsh (in press) – cost-benefits are as reported in his paper.

References

Baker, K., et al. (1995). *'Violence Prevention Through Informal Socialisation: An Evaluation of the South Baltimore Youth Centre.'* Studies on Crime and Crime Prevention, vol. 4, no. 1. National Council for Crime Prevention: Stockholm, Sweden.

Bright, J., (1997). 'Turning the tide: crime, community and prevention.' Demos: London.

Capaldi, D.M., and Patterson, G.R., (1996). 'Can violent offenders be distinguished from frequent offenders: Prediction from childhood to adolescence.' Journal of Research in Crime and Delinquency, 33, pp 206-231.

Conduct Problems Prevention Research Group, (1992). 'A Developmental and Clinical Model for the Prevention of Conduct Disorder: The FAST Track Program'. Development and Psychopathology, vol. 4, pp 509-527.

Dishion, T.J., et al. (1992). 'An Experimental Test of the Coercion Model: Linking Theory, Measurement and Intervention.' In: McCord, J. and Tremblay, R.E. (eds) *"Preventing Anti-Social Behaviour: Interventions from Birth Through Adolescence"*. New York: Guildford Press.

Dodge, K.A., (1993). 'The Future of Research on the Treatment of Conduct Disorder'. Development and Psychopathology, vol. 5, pp 311-319.

Dryfoos, J.G., (1990). *Adolescents at risk*. New York: Oxford University Press.

Farrington, D., (1993). 'Understanding and Preventing Bullying'. In: Tonry, M. (ED) Crime and Justice. vol. 17. University of Chicago Press.

Farrington, D., (1996). *'Understanding and Preventing Youth Crime'*. Joseph Rowntree Foundation: York.

Gottfredson, D.C., (1987) 'An Evaluation of an Organisation Development Approach to Reducing School Disorder.' Evaluation Review 11, pp 739-763.

Gottfredson, D., (1997) 'School-Based Crime Prevention' In: Sherman, L. W., et al. *"Preventing Crime: What Works, What Doesn't, What's Promising"*. US Department of Justice: Washington.

Gottfredson, D.C., and Gottfredson, G.D., (1986). *'The School Action Effectiveness Study: final report'*. Baltimore: John Hopkins University.

Graham, J., and Bennett, T., (1995). *'Crime Prevention Strategies in Europe and North America.'* HEUNI: Helsinki.

Graham, J., and Bowling, B., (1995). *'Young People and Crime'.* Home Office Research Study, No. 145. London: HMSO.

Graham, J., and Utting, D., (1996) 'Families, Schools and Criminality Prevention'. In: Bennett, T. (ed) *"Preventing Crime and Disorder: Targeting Strategies and Responsibilities."* Institute of Criminology, University of Cambridge: Cambridge.

Greenwood, et al. (1996). *'Diverting Children from a Life of Crime: Measuring Costs and Benefits.'* Rand Corporation: Santa Monica, California.

Hawkins, J.D., and Catalano, R.F., (1992) *'Communities That Care.'* Jossey Bass: San Fransisco.

Hawkins, J.D., et al. (1992). 'The Seattle Social Development Project: Effects of the first four years on protective factors and problem behaviours'. In: McCord, J. and Tremblay, R.E. (eds) *"Preventing Anti-social Behaviour: Interventions from Birth through Adolescence."* New York: Guildford Press.

Home Office (1987). *'Criminal careers of those born in 1953: Persistent offenders and desistance.'* Home Office Statistical Bulletin No. 35/87. London: HMSO

Karoly L.A., et.al. (1998) *Investing in our children.* RAND Corporation: Santa Monica, California.

Kazdin, A.E., Siegel, T.C., and Bass, D., (1992). 'Cognitive Problem Solving Skills Training and Parent Management Training in the Treatment of Antisocial Behaviour in Children'. *Journal of Consulting and Clinical Psychology,* vol. 60, no. 5, 733-47.

Lally, J.R., et al. (1988) 'More Pride, Less Delinquency: Findings from the ten year follow-up study of the Syracuse University Family Development Research Program'. *Zero-to-three,* vol. 8, no. 4, pp 13-18.

O'Donnell, J., et al. (1995) 'Preventing School Failure, Drug Use and Delinquency Among Low-income Children: Long-term Intervention in Elementary Schools'. *American Journal of Orthopsychiatry,* vol. 65 (1). pp 87-100.

Olds, D., et al. (1997). 'Long Term Effects of Home Visitation on Maternal Life Course and Child Abuse and Neglect: Fifteen Year Follow-up of a Randomized Trial'. The Journal of the American Medical Association, August 27, vol. 278, pp 637-643.

Olweus, D., (1990). 'Bullying Among Schoolchildren'. In: Hurrelmann, K. and Losel, F. (eds) *'Health Hazards in Adolescence.'* Berlin: De Gruyter.

Olweus, D., (1991). 'Bully/victim Problems Among Schoolchildren: Basic Facts and Effects of a School Based Intervention programme'. In: Pepler, D.J. and Rubin, K.H. (eds) *'The Development and Treatment of Childhood Aggression'.* Hillsdale, NJ: Erlbaum.

Pitts, J., and Smith, P., (1995). *'Preventing School Bullying.'* Crime Prevention and Detection Series, no. 63, Police Research Group. London: Home Office.

Reid, J.B., et al. (1994). *'A Universal Prevention Strategy for Conduct Disorder: Some Preliminary Findings'.* Paper presented to SRCAP Conference, June 1994, London.

Schweinhart, L.J., and Weikart, D.P., (1993). *'A Summary of Significant Benefits: the High/Scope Perry Pre-school Study through age 27'.* High/Scope Press: Ypsilanti/Michigan.

Sherman, L.W., (1997). 'Family-Based Crime Prevention'. In: Sherman, L. W., et al. *"Preventing Crime: What Works, What Doesn't, What's Promising".* US Department of Justice: Washington.

Sherman, L. W., et al. (1997). *"Preventing Crime: What Works, What Doesn't, What's Promising".* US Department of Justice: Washington.

Smith, P.K., and Sharp, S., (1994). *'School Bullying.'* London: Routledge.

Tremblay, R.E., et al. (1995). 'A Bimodal Preventive Intervention for Disruptive Kindergarten Boys: Its Impact Through Mid-Adolescence.' Journal of Consulting and Clinical Psychology, vol. 63, no. 4, pp 560-568.

Utting, D., (1996) *'Reducing Criminality Among Young People: A Sample of Relevant Programmes in the United Kingdom.'* Home Office Research Study, No. 161. London: HMSO.

Utting, D., Bright, J., and Henricson, C., (1993). *'Crime and the family'.* Family Policy Studies Centre. Occasional Paper 16. London.

Welsh, B., (In press). 'Economic Costs and Benefits of Primary Prevention of Delinquency and Later Offending: A Review of the Literature.' in J. W. Coid and D. P. Farrington (eds.), *Early Prevention of Adult Antisocial Behaviour,* Cambridge: Cambridge Univeristy Press.

3 Situational crime prevention: effectiveness of local initiatives

Paul Ekblom

Introduction

This chapter deals with Situational Crime Prevention (SCP), focusing on what can be achieved through local interventions. Action at a national level, particularly the avoidance of future "crime harvests", is dealt with in more detail in Chapter 4. Examples of costs and savings are provided to indicate cost-effectiveness. Risks and infrastructure issues are also addressed.

The previous chapter of this report dealt with promoting a less criminal society, partly by initiatives aimed at offenders or potential offenders. SCP, as its name implies, does not aim to affect *offenders'* propensities or motives. It takes these as given and, proceeding from an analysis of the circumstances giving rise to particular crimes, it introduces specific changes to influence the offender's *decision* or ability to commit these crimes at particular places and times. Thus it seeks to make criminal actions less attractive to offenders rather than relying on detection, sanctions or reducing criminality through, for example, improvements in society or its institutions. These contrasting approaches are discussed in later chapters.

The approach can be applied to any environment, product or service. All are potential targets for crime. The main approaches to SCP are listed in Table 3.1. Examples include:

- target hardening (e.g. strengthening coin boxes in telephone kiosks);

- controlling access to crime targets (e.g. entry phones);

- surveillance (e.g. burglar alarms, CCTV, improved street lighting);

- target removal (e.g. removable car radios);

Table 3.1 Situational crime prevention: examples of the main approaches

1. Target hardening	**9. Target removal**
• Strengthened coin boxes in telephone kiosks	• Removable car radios
	• Women's refuges
• Steering column locks on cars	• Phonecards to eliminate cash in
• Anti-robbery screens in banks, etc.	• public pay phones
2. Controlling access to crime targets	**10. Property identification**
• Fencing around flats to reduce vandalism	• Property marking
	• Vehicle licensing
• Entry phones	• Cattle branding
• Caretakers for multi-occupancy buildings	**11. Reducing temptation**
3. Deflecting offenders from targets	• Gender-neutral phone listings
• Segregating fans at football matches	• Off-street parking
• Pub location	• Rapid repair
• Closing streets to stop cruising for prostitutes	**12. Taking away benefits**
	• Ink merchandise tags
4. Controlling crime facilitators	• Graffiti cleaning
• Photographs on credit cards	• Disabling stolen mobile phones/videos
• Toughened glasses and bottles in pubs	**13. Setting rules**
• Passwords for mobile phones	• Customs declaration
5. Screening entrances and exits	• Harassment codes
• Automatic ticket gates at stations	• Hotel registration
• Baggage screening at airports	**14. Alerting conscience**
• Merchandise tags in shops	• Roadside speedometers
6. Formal surveillance	• "Shoplifting is stealing" signs
• Speeding and red light traffic cameras	• "Idiots drink and drive" signs
• Burglar alarms	**15. Controlling factors that undermine constraint**
• City guards	
7. Surveillance by employees	• Law controlling drinking age
• Locate pay phones where employees can see	• V-chip in TVs to block violent programmes
• Park attendants	• Controlling alcohol at public events
• CCTV systems	**16. Making compliance easier**
8. Natural surveillance	• Easy library checkout to discourage book theft
• 'Defensible space' environmental design	• Public lavatories
• Improved street lighting	• Litter bins
• 'Cocoon' neighbourhood watch	

Note:

    Facilitating implementation of these various activities comes under the policy remit of a wide range of central and local government departments, agencies and private concerns.

Source: Adapted from Clarke (1997)

- property identification (e.g. property marking);

- reducing temptation (e.g. gender-neutral phone listings);

- alerting conscience (e.g. "Shoplifting is stealing" signs);

- controlling factors that undermine constraint (e.g. alcohol at public events); and,

- making compliance easier (e.g. improving checkouts).

Changing the immediate crime situation in these different ways involves three fundamental approaches: *deterrence* (which makes the crime seem more risky), *discouragement* (which makes it harder, or less rewarding) and removing excuses (which awakens conscience, as in the example of 'shoplifting is stealing'). These involve systematically changing a crime *target* that is vulnerable and attractive, *crime preventers* who are absent or incapable, *crime promoters* who are negligent or deliberate or an unhelpful environment.

Implementing SCP

SCP can work both *reactively* to an emerging crime problem and in *anticipation*, through crime impact analyses on proposed new policies, practices or products (to assess whether they may inadvertently increase opportunities for crime), and through incorporating prevention within the design process. It can operate both *locally* (e.g. on a specific disorder problem in a particular housing estate) or *nationally/internationally* (e.g. on the vulnerability of a particular model of car). A host of different sectors are involved in implementing SCP – these include the general public, the private sector, local government, and voluntary and statutory agencies. It can be implemented by people protecting themselves (or protecting those for whom they have some specific responsibility – such as housing associations on behalf of their tenants), by those with a 'service duty' (police or security guards) and by those with a wider 'duty of care' (e.g. manufacturers ensuring their goods cannot be easily stolen or used to facilitate crime). The level of expertise needed can range from routine common-sense precautions to highly-developed technical controls in computer-based financial systems.

The range of offences susceptible to SCP

SCP can apply to every kind of crime, not just to 'opportunistic' or acquisitive property offences. Case studies (Clarke, 1997) show successful applications to more calculated or deeply-motivated crimes and ones committed by hardened offenders (e.g. aircraft hijacking, commercial robbery, homicide, sexual harassment and violence). Major fraud can also be covered.

SCP in a wider crime reduction context

SCP can be implemented in a range of contexts. In an informal context, routine precautions taken by householders, businesses etc. complement informal social control. Both contribute an unknown, but probably very significant, amount to crime reduction. The formal contexts in which preventive activity can take place include:

- *police crime prevention survey and advisory service* – this has traditionally been driven by requests from the public or businesses;

- *community-oriented prevention* – where the community as a whole is protected or takes action together on a specific problem and where the mechanism for prevention is provided by the community. This is described more fully in Chapter 5;

- *community safety* – where prevention of crime is seen as integral to maintaining or improving quality of life, sustaining an environment where people can pursue their lives as free as possible from hazards such as crime;

- *crime control* – where actions are taken to keep crime and disorder at or below tolerable levels and to stop the growth of particular crime problems and the number and sophistication of offenders; and,

- *reducing crime through wider social and economic policy* – e.g. encouraging reduction of premiums for improved home security (discussed more fully in Chapter 4).

Strengths of SCP

The strengths of SCP have emerged from evaluation studies over a long period (e.g. Clarke, 1997). It accords with common-sense self-protection, which it can enhance and build upon. The interventions are highly focused. They prevent crime in specific places, against specific products, etc. and can bypass intractable social problems unresponsive to other approaches, complementing those which treat or incapacitate offenders. Potentially, they protect a wider set of crime targets and are proof against replacement of offenders, avoiding harmful side-effects of approaches that lead to confrontation with the police, labelling, embitterment and criminal education of offenders.

Removing temptation through SCP may have a 'multiplier' effect if it prevents crimes such as shop theft – a 'classic' entry to a criminal career. There may be a point at which the protection afforded by SCP broadens out from influencing specific tactical decisions by offenders to the more strategic one of desisting from offending. Typically SCP needs a short time to implement and impact. This has many advantages, including prevention of runaway growth in crime (see below).

Preventing runaway growth

Under some circumstances, specific crimes against specific targets can enjoy runaway growth. One study (Ekblom, 1987) illustrates cost-effectiveness in this context. There was a wave of robberies of London sub post-offices, increasing from 70 in 1980 to 250 in 1981. Following an initiative to introduce anti-bandit screens, robberies rapidly declined and by 1986 had fallen back to about 100 per year. Investment in improved security was judged to have provided an annual return over the period 1983-86 *of a third to a half of the initial capital outlay*. If benefits ceased at that point this would still amount to a return on investment of £1.30-£2 per pound spent. Presumably, if SCP had not been implemented, the growth in robberies would eventually have halted - but at a higher point. But this might have required more drastic means, like closure of post-offices. Costing these significant 'hypothetical harmful consequences avoided' is challenging.

SCP can exploit the 'targetability' of crime problems – repeat victimisation, hot spots, hot products – to increase cost-effectiveness. More generally, measures of action are *relatively* easy to link to outcome. Evaluation results thus feed directly into community safety strategies.

SCP: assessment of risks

Process evaluations are particularly well-developed in situational prevention. They indicate, from a practical perspective, what does not work and when. They suggest that none of the potential problems are inevitable and can usually be minimised in practice. **But to ensure that the benefits of SCP consistently outweigh the costs – which they can do by a wide margin – means investing in the quality of practitioners, and the infrastructure of information and training.**

Possible limitations

A number of potential problems need to be considered:

- critics of SCP claim that displacement of offending to other, less-well protected targets, times and places can reduce the gains. Examples can readily be provided, **but recent reviews suggest this is limited** (e.g. Hesseling, 1994). Often offenders give protected areas a wider berth than necessary, creating a "diffusion of benefits" that offset or replace displacement effects;

- most effective SCP methods grow obsolete. This happens more quickly if they work by *illusorily* heightening offenders' sense of risk (e.g. CCTV cameras with few back-up staff to monitor them). In the longer term, offenders develop countermeasures. Social/ technological change brings new targets (laptop computers, mobile phones), tools (cordless drills) and ways of disseminating criminal techniques (Internet);

- as with other crime reduction techniques, there are few universal remedies. What works is generally context-dependent. Additionally, without adequate expertise or quality assurance, SCP is especially prone to fads and fashions, slick salesmanship and the use of 'cook book' approaches (where techniques that succeed in one setting are replicated in others without regard to the changed context); and,

- *'Action at a distance'* is often needed when those responsible for reducing crime have to get others to implement interventions in a local context (see Chapters 4 and 5).

Possible harmful consequences

The evidence for harmful consequences of SCP is scant. However where the potential to do harm is identified it may need to be 'designed out' or managed. Although displacement from relatively 'benign' offending to more serious crime is probably very limited, if it occurs it needs to be countered. Where design or implementation are carried out insensitively, this could increase fear; limit the freedom of *legitimate* users (of products, environments or services), foster an attitude of victim-blaming; and introduce an unpleasant, fortified and beleaguered environment. Positive action is therefore needed to avoid the occurrence of any of these.

Some types of intervention may be perceived to threaten privacy (e.g. misuse of CCTV and abuse of ID registration). Research has shown that people are prepared to accept the legitimate use of CCTV surveillance in shops or public places but are resistant to compulsory identification. However private security firms with unskilled/badly-supervised 'watchmen' need to be monitored to avoid abuse.

SCP can create conflicts with safety or convenience and careful design and management are required to avoid this. False alarms (about 90% of alarm incidents attended by police are false) have an opportunity cost of police time and inflict noise pollution on the public. One (not very reliable) US cost-benefit study (Hakim et al., 1995) suggested a *loss* of $0.35 for each dollar invested in alarms. New technology and procedures should improve matters.

Distribution of benefits and harm

The way in which different groups or individuals benefit from, or are harmed by, preventive measures requires careful consideration (Field, 1993):

- laissez-faire SCP can lead to inequity, with displacement of crime from the better-off to those less able to protect themselves or obtain publicly funded resources (see Chapter 5 for more discussion of this);

- undesirable effects of SCP, such as noise pollution from car alarms, can fall on others. Local and national policy steers are needed on these issues;

- adequate levels of protection from the individual's perspective may not secure crime reduction benefits for society as a whole; and,

- where crime problems are 'externalised' (i.e. where those who create the opportunity are not those who suffer the consequential crimes), sanctions could be introduced to encourage closing the loophole.

SCP – scale of impact on crime

Gross impact

Evaluations of SCP have shown varying success. High-quality demonstration projects and evaluation reviews focusing on success can indicate the maximum impact of SCP when appropriately targeted, designed and implemented. A representative range here would be **a 40–70 per cent reduction in expected levels of crime**. This would be a gross figure of impact in the targeted area, excluding displacement (see below). The development of SCP through the Home Office and other agencies has perhaps been accompanied by evaluation more than most other crime reduction approaches. But even so, only a few indicate results that may be generalisable to similar settings at other times and places (specifically what Sherman et al., 1997, regard as promising or better – see Annex A).

Reliable evaluations of large-scale implementations (as distinct from development or demonstration projects) are rare. This has, in particular, limited our knowledge of the effectiveness of initiatives involving less sophisticated targeting and planning. One of the exceptions to this was the Home Office's evaluation of the mainly situational action against domestic burglary implemented in the Safer Cities Programme (Ekblom et al., 1996a, b). In this programme, action was implemented on a relatively large-scale in around 500 schemes over several years. The co-ordinators and practitioners had a fairly limited grasp of crime prevention methods and processes. The evaluation covered nearly 300 of the schemes using either survey or recorded crime data (or both). Figure 3.1 shows the results for surveys of 96 schemes (very similar results were obtained using recorded crime). Depending on the background burglary rate, intensity of action and the outcome measures used, impact ranged from about 10 per cent to about 30 per cent reduction in expected levels of crime. Further gains are possible: Safer Cities action largely predated the focus on repeat victimisation which promises to boost impact further; nor was the quality of action always high. We revisit the Safer Cities findings at various points below to illustrate a range of cost-effectiveness issues.

Figure 3.1 Safer Cities – Observed and expected domestic burglary prevalence after preventive action

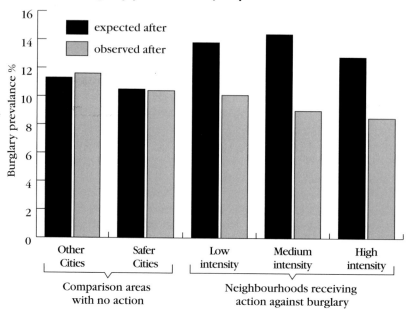

There is evidence that combining SCP with other types of action produces gains over and above what could be expected on the basis of their performance when delivered separately. This was evident, for example, in the Safer Cities programme when local crime reduction strategies against a **range of crime problems** combined SCP with offender-oriented action. Similar synergistic gains might be expected if SCP were combined with conventional policing, e.g. crackdowns on 'fences' or high rate offenders. But enthusiasm for all-embracing approaches should be tempered by selective pursuit of cost-effective combinations of preventive methods.

Businesses can, of course, contribute directly to crime reduction (and, where this is the case, the role of government may simply be to promote and encourage their contribution). A recent evaluation of the predominantly situational measures adopted since 1990 to control a rising problem of fraud with plastic cards has shown major success (Levi and Handley, 1998). Charge card, cheque card, credit card and debit card fraud in the UK almost halved (from around £120million) over the period 1991–95. The ratio of fraud to turnover on sales of goods fell from 0.34 per cent to 0.09 per cent. To the direct financial benefits of reduced losses must be added the preservation of confidence in the banking system.

Net impact

Displacement of crime to other targets would reduce the net impact of SCP, but *diffusion of benefit* would increase it (as discussed above). The Safer Cities burglary evaluation found a range of effects under different conditions. Displacement to neighbouring areas appeared to happen when the level of anti-burglary action delivered was of low intensity. Where the action was of moderate or higher intensity, diffusion of benefit seemed to outweigh displacement in the immediately-surrounding areas at least. Low intensity action against *burglary* also appeared to induce 'crime switch' to *other property offences* in the action area but with greater intensity the protection against burglary extended to reduce the other property offences too.

Cost-effectiveness of SCP

Studies of cost-effectiveness of SCP are extremely rare. A recent review (Welsh and Farrington, in press, 1998) listed only 13 (including the Safer Cities evaluation) which included an assessment of monetary costs and benefits. A summary of eight which they examined in detail is shown in Table 3.2. The ratios of costs to benefits shown in the table should be seen as predominantly illustrative of the range to be found within SCP. As the authors put it, "No attempt has been made to determine which of the studies provides the most favourable economic return on investment, because of the small number of studies reviewed and the varied methodological rigour of the programme evaluations and economic analyses." To get a fuller picture we have to switch between in-practice and in-principle assessments (including the material on strengths and limitations already covered); and to draw on evaluations that are not as reliable as might be wished.

Table 3.2 Estimated costs and benefits obtained in situational prevention studies

Authors	Crimes targeted	Context of intervention	Method of intervention	Cost-benefit ratio[1]
Cirel et al. 1977	Burglary	Home (Seattle)	Neighbourhood Watch	0.4
Ekblom et al. 1996	Burglary	Home (Safer Cities)	Target hardening plus (benefits calculated over 2 years)	1.8 (higher if targeted on higher crime areas)
Forrester et al. 1990	Burglary	Home (Kirkholt)	Target removal (coin meters) + repeat victimisation	5
Clarke & McGrath 1990	Robbery	Betting shop	Target hardening	1.7
Painter & Farrington 1997, 1998	Property and personal crime in general	Residential streets and footpaths	Natural surveillance (street lighting)	3.1 - 4.7
Skilton 1988	Vandalism	Public housing estate	Employee surveillance - concierge	1.4
van Andel 1989	Vandalism, toll fraud, assault	Public transport	Formal surveillance - special transport officials	0.3

Source: Adapted from Welsh and Farrington (1998).

Notes:
The studies shown in the above table are those for which Welsh and Farrington (1998) presented detailed economic analyses. The cost-benefit ratios were calculated by Welsh and Farrington (using data available in the published source) on the basis of preventing criminal events. The period over which benefits accrued is not always clear from Welsh and Farrington's cost-benefit analysis. It is advisable to note the authors' health warning: 'No attempt has been made to determine which of the studies provides the most favourable economic return on investment, because of the small number of studies reveiwed and the varied methodological rigour of the programme evaluations and economic analyses.'

Cost-effectiveness of SCP at the design stage – anticipation

If SCP is applied at the *design stage* of, for example, houses, cars, consumer electronics, retail electronic point-of-sale systems, or the benefit system it can be very cost-effective in heading off a harvest of crime (see Chapter 4). Sometimes the only investment required is well-informed thought to reveal a vulnerability that hindsight would make painfully obvious (e.g. putting more steeply sloping lids on wheeled refuse bins to prevent their use as climbing aids). Failure to tackle vulnerability at this stage could bequeath owners, users, and society as a whole, a crime *legacy* of years in the case of cars, or decades in the case of buildings.

Evidence for the effectiveness (if not yet the cost-effectiveness) of Government-orchestrated local action at the design stage comes from the Dutch 'Secured Housing' scheme (Scherpenisse, 1997). For approval, developers' projects must meet standards covering residents' participation, neighbourhood management, home watch, and building design including layout of rooms and entrances and target-hardening. An evaluation in Rotterdam showed a 70 per cent reduction in burglaries after one year between those new houses involved in the programme, and those not.

Cost-effectiveness of SCP at the remedial stage

With *remedial* security measures, in the Safer Cities evaluation, careful definition of anti-burglary action made it possible to estimate the gross cost of achieving impact. Two independent outcome measures (recorded crime and surveys) gave remarkably close estimates of £300–£900 per burglary prevented, based on an assumption of a duration of impact of only two years. The lesser figure was for implementation in higher-risk areas typical of cities. The higher figure was for areas of national average burglary risk. These were set against estimated financial costs of burglary to victims and the state of about £1,100.

The evaluation estimated that the Safer Cities burglary action, which was predominantly situational, cost some £4 million (+£2.6 million leverage) in *direct* anti-burglary scheme funding. If we add the extra costs of Safer Cities action against *other* crimes and the Programme's administrative overheads, the *total* cost would be about £31 million. This prevented some 56,000 burglaries whose cost to victims and the state would have been £62 million. Therefore the benefits from burglary reduction alone were twice that spent on the entire programme (which tackled a much wider range of crime problems). Over the whole programme, displacement associated with burglary schemes was judged to have been at least balanced by diffusion of benefit although this remains a 'soft' estimate. Social and psychological savings were additional. A cost-effectiveness trade-off on *intensity of action* is illustrated below.

> ### *Cost-effectiveness trade-off on intensity of action versus coverage*
>
> Reduction in burglary risk through Safer Cities action was greater where there was more intense burglary action, but to achieve these bigger falls cost disproportionately more. 'Marginal cost' estimates per *extra* prevented burglary, achieved by starting up schemes with more funds, ranged from about £1,100 in the highest risk areas to about £3,300 in the lower risk ones. In gross monetary terms, crime prevention agencies with a limited budget, as in Safer Cities (£250,000/year/city in SC 1, £100,000/year/city in SC 2) might make their money go further by spending less money per household. This would not substantially reduce the *direct* impact of the action in the targeted areas because the mere presence of even modest action seemed to have a strong effect (probably by rendering the whole area less attractive to burglars). This 'thin-spreading' would therefore be worth considering. But the disadvantages of doing so would include negation of the crime reduction through displacement to other areas or to other crimes, and a failure to alleviate people's worry about burglary or how they judge their neighbourhood. (All of these problems were avoided only when action was more intense.) It might also be especially vulnerable to offender habituation, shortening the duration of impact.

Other benefits and costs

Many SCP initiatives also aim to reduce fear of crime. Some have apparently succeeded. But little research has assessed direct *behavioural* benefits of SCP on quality of life, such as increasing people's use and enjoyment of their locality – or its contribution to social/economic regeneration. From a business perspective, reductions in fraud, assault, robbery, criminal damage etc. which SCP in particular may deliver can yield benefits in terms of increased profitability, improvements in the conditions of staff, avoidance of serious business interruptions, and user confidence. The wider community can then gain through reduced prices and improved investment in facilities, and avoid the flight of commerce from high-crime locations.

SCP – how much of UK's crime could it prevent?

The limits to how much of the UK's crime problems could be tackled by SCP are not theoretical, but practical and related to cost-effectiveness. SCP has probably contributed to a major reduction in aircraft hijacking, at a great price, but one worth paying given the costs of *not* doing so.

> ### *Targeting higher-crime areas: a trade-off between coverage versus cost-effectiveness*
>
> Two alternative estimates were calculated of possible *national* impact of Safer Cities-type burglary action:
>
> a) targeting higher-risk areas amounting to a tenth of the country's 20 million households gives a 5.5% reduction in national burglary rates and gross financial benefits about *two-and-a-half times as great as the spend* (£94 million benefits for a spend of £38 million).; and,
>
> b) covering half the country's households reduces the national burglary rate by nearly an eighth but financial benefits are only a third more than spend (£205 million benefits for a spend of £151 million).

More sophisticated targeting strategies could improve returns in both cases but would require investment to provide the necessary information base. At the end of the day, balancing targeting, coverage, cost-effectiveness and fair distribution of funding is a matter of policy choice.

Attempts to project impact nation-wide are rare for any approach to prevention. This has, however, been done with the Safer Cities burglary prevention results. The results (below) also illustrate the tradeoff between extent of coverage of the nation's crime problems, and cost-effectiveness.

Some of the other areas where SCP prospects are good at the national scale are discussed in Chapter 4.

SCP – the infrastructure to make it work

Good SCP requires more than the resources that are needed simply to implement individual initiatives:

- for those SCP methods that rely on risk to deter the offender, the chief hidden ingredient is a Criminal Justice System efficient enough to make the risks credible. This means SCP must work in concert with conventional crime control. But it may make substantial savings on the latter and confer important additional benefits;

- good data are needed to target preventive action efficiently and to monitor, tune and evaluate the action once implemented;

- quality assurance - ensuring that schemes and evaluations adhere to crime prevention principles and are appropriate requires co-ordination, supervision and monitoring of large numbers of local initiatives. This effort can be reduced if SCP is developed as a professional discipline;

- local practitioners need training and support. They must be sufficiently expert to tailor solutions to local contexts, and to tune their first attempts in the light of experience;

- any professional discipline of prevention needs a substantial programme of basic research and information. It also needs demonstration projects and reliable evaluation to produce practical knowledge of the working principles of SCP; and,

- evaluation itself requires further investment to yield sufficient reliable material. It needs routine and timely information both on *outcome* and on *action outputs* disaggregated to a local level.

Conclusions

SCP can contribute significantly to crime control. When properly targeted and sensitively implemented SCP interventions work and are cost-effective. Removing the opportunity to offend complements approaches dealing with offenders' propensity and motivation to commit crime through the formal CJS and outside it. In particular SCP offers coverage of a wide range of crime problems that other approaches may not reach; highly-focused interventions that promise quick wins; and the chance to circumvent, in the short term, intractable social problems which may be generating crime. SCP is not a recipe for abolishing law enforcement and treatment for convicted offenders. Rather, it can be seen as a way of making enforcement more of a "response of last resort" to crime. Successful SCP – particularly where properly-publicised – may help tone down public pressure for exclusive reliance on retributive crime control.

SCP does not involve heroic interventions, high-speed police chases or the drama of the court – so its appeal (like that of public health) has to be more rationally argued. Some of this appeal can flow from technological wizardry and outwitting offenders. It can also be seen as an element of any 'responsible society'. If people and institutions do not protect *themselves* when offered suitable guidance they will incur significant costs and harmful consequences, encouraging offenders' careers with easy rewards. Simply shifting these costs and consequences onto others does nothing to discourage offenders. If people and institutions do not take reasonable care to avoid generating opportunities for crime against *others*, they are 'exporting' crime problems to the rest of society (in a similar way to the creation of environmental pollution).

References

Cirel, P., Evans, P., McGillis, D. and Whitcomb, D., (1977). *An exemplary project: Community crime prevention.* Seattle, Washington: National Criminal Justice Reference Service.

Clarke, R., (1997). *Situational Crime Prevention: Successful Case Studies (2nd Edn).* Albany, N.Y.: Harrow and Heston

Clarke, R., and McGrath, G., (1990). Cash reduction and robbery prevention in Australian betting shops. *Security Journal,* 1:160 163.

Ekblom. P., (1987). *Preventing robberies at sub-Post Offices: an evaluation of a security initiati*ve. Home Office CPU Paper 9. London: Home Office.

Ekblom, P., Law, H., and Sutton, M. (1996a) *Safer Cities and domestic burglary.* HORS 164. London: Home Office.

Ekblom, P., Law, H. and Sutton, M., (1996b) *Domestic burglary schemes in the Safer Cities Programme* Research Findings 42. London: Home Office.

Field, S., (1993). Crime prevention and the costs of auto theft: an economic analysis. *Crime Prevention Studies,* 1:69-92.

Forrester, D., Frenz, S., O'Connell, M., and Pease, K., (1990). *The Kirkholt burglary prevention project: Phase II.* Home Office CPU Paper 23. London: Home Office.

Hakim, S., Gaffney, M., Rengert, G., and Schachmurove, J., (1995). Costs and benefits of alarms to the community: Burglary patterns and security measures in Tredyffrin township, Pennsylvania. *Security Journal,* 6:197204.

Hesseling, R., (1994). Displacement: a review of the empirical literature. *Crime Prevention Studies,* 3:197230.

Levi, M., and Handley, J., (1998) *The prevention of plastic and cheque fraud revisited.* HORS 182. London: Home Office.

Painter, K., and Farrington, D., (1997). The crime reducing effect of improved street lighting: The Dudley Project. In R. Clarke (Ed), *Situational crime prevention: Successful case studies* (2nd Edn), pp209-226. Albany, New York: Harrow and Heston.

Painter, K., and Farrington, D., (1998, in press). Street lighting and crime: diffusion of benefits in the Stoke-on-Trent Project. In K. Painter and N. Tilley (Eds.) *Crime Prevention Studies*, vol. [x]. Monsey, N.Y.: Criminal Justice Press.

Scherpenisse, R., (1997). *The police label for secured housing: Initial results in the Netherlands.* Paper presented to the European Union Conference, 'Crime Prevention Towards a European Level' Noordwijk, Netherlands.

Sherman, L. W., et.al. (1997). *Preventing Crime: What works, what doesn't, what's promising.* Office of Justice Programs Research Report, US Department of Justice: Washington D.C.

Shover, N., (1996). *Great pretenders: Pursuits and careers of persistent thieves.* London: Westview Press/Harper Collins.

Skilton, M., (1988). *A better reception: The development of concierge schemes.* London: Estate Action and Department of the Environment.

van Andel, H., (1989). Crime prevention that works: The care of public transport in The Netherlands. *British Journal of Criminology*, 29:47-56.

Welsh, B., and Farrington, D.P., (1998). Value for money? A review of the costs and benefits of Situational Crime Prevention. *British Journal of Criminology*, vol.38 (in press).

4 Changing the context of crime prevention

Ken Pease

Introduction

This chapter reviews past research and draws conclusions on changes that might be made to the way government, manufacturers and the public think and behave so as to reduce opportunities for crime. It draws on the framework for situational prevention presented in Chapter 3, placing particular emphasis on the need to increase personal and organisational incentives for crime prevention. Examples of how to react to new products and services are given.

Policy as a way of manipulating incentives

An important part of government activity is the way policy aims to change people's behaviour through incentives. The manipulation of tax, benefits, opportunities and regulation is an integral part of government policy in many areas. In transport policy there have been recent "hard" incentives towards less use of private cars by increasing fuel prices above inflation and "soft" incentives with even the main motorist organisations (AA and RAC) voicing concern about the non-sustainability of increasing road use. In energy policy the government plans to reduce VAT for some energy-saving household expenditure.

In the area of crime prevention such policy initiatives are rare. However, when people or organisations want, or are induced to want, to reduce crime, they seem largely to do so with little difficulty:

- HMV successfully reduced crime in its Oxford Street store when the threat was made to reduce police services (Ekblom, 1986);

- the Department of Social Security reduced benefit fraud when it recognised the scale of the problem (see, for example, Rowlingson et al., 1997);

- the UK plastic card industry (collaborating through APACS) took effective steps to reduce fraud levels in the early 1990s (see Levi et al., 1991; Levi and Handley, 1998). This happened before it was commercially rational to do so, as a result of pressure from politicians;

- the UK car industry improved security on new cars following the publication of the Car Theft Index by the Home Office in 1992 (Houghton, 1992); and,

- the Swedish security firm Stralfors were induced by the Swedish government to introduce the controlled supply of laminated number plates, with bar-coded car details, which ensure that the registration number does belong to the car in which it is placed.

However, there are occasions when action to reduce crime results in an effective penalty to the person or organisation taking the action:

i) there can be increased local taxation of shops after security enhancement which increases the shop's value;

ii) insurance lowers the optimal level of protection for society as a whole. In the present commercial climate it is possible to ally low security with insurance protection; and,

iii) the Driver Vehicle and Licensing Authority is in a position to organise vehicle licensing in ways less prone to crime. However, as DVLA income is unaffected by fraud levels, there is no financial incentive for them to reduce those levels.

There are also circumstances under which *individual* citizens would *not* involve themselves in crime-reduction efforts (Hope, 1995) when:

i) the perceived risks or costs of voluntary participation outweigh its apparent benefits;

ii) neighbourhood involvement has opportunity costs;

iii) marginal additions in participation are thought not to produce commensurate reductions in risk; and,

iv) a critical mass of other citizens has been reached which allows the individual to enjoy the benefits of collective action without contributing to it.

To these may be added organisational factors leading to institutions not involving themselves in crime reduction. These include where:

i) institutional units would not themselves benefit from their crime-cutting achievements;

ii) crime losses as a percentage of turnover are below a threshold at which it is deemed worthy of action; and,.

iii) an institution's audit systems fail to separately identify crime-related losses.

Lessons from research

Criminology as an aid to crime reduction policy has not always helped since there has generally been a neglect of individual motivation in research. This has led to a greater emphasis on structures than on personal incentives. Criminology has also generally favoured analysis in hindsight over the riskier business of prediction.

However, good frameworks for crime prevention have now been produced (e.g. Ekblom, 1997) which emphasise the evolutionary nature of crime and responses to it through design tactics and strategy:

i) R&D must be continuous to keep ahead of obsolescence. It must be combined with a national 'surveillance system' enabling rapid response to the identification of emergent crime targets, and new tools and methods of offending;

ii) implementing *anticipatory* design would require investment in research, production of quality design guides, private/public design services covering national and local requirements, and an accreditation system. The police currently fill some of this role, and the 'Secure By Design' scheme and British Standards provide some certification. But a thorough review might be appropriate. European moves (CEN) are afoot on this. There may be particular lessons to learn from the Danish and Dutch approaches, the latter involving partnerships with insurance companies, and mutual agreements by police and designers/producers to improve how problems are addressed; and,

iii) publicity is also important in fostering a suitable crime prevention climate and changing the moral climate on responsibility for creating criminal opportunities.

is also recent research (Mann and Sutton, 1998) into crime prevention implications of the growth of activity on the Internet. Other lessons from recent research into electronic developments imply that change will be non-linear:

i)   the growth of e-commerce and its problems for security of payment systems (Schwartz, 1997);

ii) the globalisation of financial systems and its threat to national tax revenues (Platt, 1997);

iii) the availability of music and text via the Net and the copyright implications of that (Browning, 1997); and,

iv) the role of the Internet in political terrorism/activism (Bennahum, 1997) and the scope for electronic warfare (Craddock, 1997).

When considering the future we need to plan explicitly for innovation. Physical and social innovations typically go through three phases:

i)   innovation with indifference to crime consequences;

ii) crime harvests as a consequence of (i); and,

iii) the retrofitting of partial solutions to (ii).

A historic example of this is the introduction of smooth-edged coins, followed by coin clipping and the eventual introduction of milled edges (Ekblom, 1995). A more recent example is the proliferation of mobile phones, which are high value, small volume, anonymous communication devices easily convertible to criminal use. Many aspects of their manufacture, distribution and call patterns could have been used to limit their utility as stolen goods or tools in drug sales. Some of these measures are now being belatedly taken (Roberts 1996).

Who pays?

Clearly it is important to ensure that innovation of goods and services should incorporate thinking about how to avoid or minimise crimes associated with them such as theft or obtaining services without payment. Individual and agency self-protection should be in the front line against crime. Not all the costs need be borne by government. Building on the evidence-base for self-protection (and disseminating the necessary information) could be a very cost-effective way to multiply the impact of limited government expenditure (provided, of course, that people have, or are given, the incentive to improve security).

Experience has shown too that governments can often find suitable 'interested parties' to fund or facilitate prevention. The *insurance* industry is one such collaborator. The *private security* industry could also be encouraged to move away from low-grade surveillance-oriented work to a more 'value-added' market position involving more sophisticated risk assessment and provision of services based on its own research.

Where businesses and other institutions generate opportunities for crime, and pay less than an appropriate share of the resulting CJS costs through their taxes, it is worth considering extending the 'polluter pays' principle. This would require development of some kind of fair and transparent way of tracking and accounting for the costs.

Suggestions for change

There is a need to consider how best to improve incentives for crime reduction and how best to respond to innovation in goods and services.

Incentives

It is important not to take for granted the wish to reduce crime among individuals and organisations and to recognise that incentives have a useful part to play. Even some police forces do not yet have clear and co-ordinated strategies for reducing crime (HM Inspector of Constabulary, 1998), although this situation should improve rapidly as a result of the duties that will be placed on local crime reduction partnerships when the Crime and Disorder Bill is enacted. Various examples in which incentives could operate to encourage crime prevention are: changes to local or national personal taxation; similar changes in corporate taxation; encouragement for the reduction of insurance premiums.

There is as yet, however, no complete list of possible incentives, evaluation of how most incentives would work in practice or of the difficulties there may be in introducing them. More work is needed on this; indeed a continuing review of incentives should be an ongoing part of central crime prevention thinking.

Effective incentives can be soft as well as hard. Matthews et al. (1998) suggest large differences between banks in rates of repeat robbery which implies that some banks are putting into place measures after one robbery to prevent the next. Similar differences exist between car models (Houghton,

1992) and no doubt other products or services. Behind-the-scenes threats to shame or to withdraw police prosecution resources can be effective, as happened with the HMV music shop mentioned earlier. A more overt approach is provided by product indices (such as the Car Theft Index). These help consumers avoid the least secure products and encourage competition between manufacturers based on their reputation for secure products. Such differences could be made public if discussion fails to secure adoption of best practice.

Routine attack testing

As stated above, we need to move to a position in which crime consequences are anticipated at the point goods or services are introduced. This will not slow the pace of innovation but simply extend the product usefulness of the first version of a new device or service. Greater emphasis is needed to identify emerging crime patterns and opportunities and for crime consequences to be addressed in Computer Aided Design packages; among the criteria for Design Council and RSA awards; and to have routine attack testing of new products (as increasingly occurs with cars and computer systems). Cost-effective structures for routine attack testing should be investigated, perhaps in pilot studies.

Sometimes it is more straightforward to forecast what is needed in crime prevention. A likely example from the near future is the coming of digital TV. From now to around 2010 set-top boxes will be usable with analogue TV. From 2000, integrated digital TVs, with high value and portability, will be introduced into UK homes. After 2010 analogue TVs will be useless. As about a quarter of burglaries involve TV theft it is likely that there will be a burglary bonanza unless some crime prevention action is taken.

It seems there is a straightforward technical solution. Digital TVs have a uniquely identifiable microprocessor which can be interrogated remotely. Stolen TVs can thus be electronically deactivated, e.g. by using a Ceefax page containing the numbers of stolen TVs which is scanned automatically at switch-on. If a TV finds its own number, it switches itself off, and remains unusable. This can be done at low cost. Some companies are moving in this direction, but Home Office, police and insurer pressure seems necessary to motivate suppliers and retailers to make it universal, and consumers to wish it to be so.

What central government can do

There are many ways in which central government can encourage prevention:

i) people and institutions are made aware of the possibilities of crime prevention;

ii) principles are intelligently applied to a wide range of specific problems;

iii) evidence-based interventions are used wherever available;

iv) market failures are corrected by acceptable application of incentives and sanctions;

v) suitable facilities and products are developed to meet market requirements; and,

vi) mechanisms are in place to detect or anticipate emergent crime problems in product design and to make crime impact statements about proposed new policies and practices.

Institutional arrangements to support these functions will be needed, to establish and maintain links at several levels for co-ordination between bodies which are sources of criminal opportunity or motivation, which are victims of crime, or which have the capacity to prevent it:

i) the *national* (and *international*) level would involve agencies, institutions and private companies with direct parts to play in implementing crime prevention at this scale; and Government departments responsible for influencing these through the relevant policy areas (such as housing, town planning, vehicle construction and design, the Internet, financial systems, retail practices, benefit systems etc.), and regulatory agencies. Encouragingly, crime control is achieving a higher profile in the DTI-led technology Foresight Programme than previously;

ii) the *local* level would, obviously, involve police, local authorities and others already identified in the 'partnership' literature and the current consultative document 'Getting to Grips with Crime', including local business interests; and,

iii) *local-national* links would be needed to ensure that crime prevention, an essentially local activity in many cases, is both working for the national interest, and fully supported by the centre.

References

Bennahum D.S., (1997) 'The Internet Revolution' *Wired* 5.4 122-173.

Browning J., (1997) 'Copyrighter's Block' *Wired* 5.5 67-104.

Craddock A., (1997) 'Netwar and Peace in the Global Village' Wired 5.5 52-226.

Ekblom P., (1986) *The Prevention of Shop Theft: An Approach through Crime Analysis.* Crime Prevention Paper 5. London: Home Office.

Eblom P., (1995) Less crime, by Design. *The Annals of the American Academy of Political and Social Science,* 539, 114-129

Ekblom P., (1997) 'Gearing up against Crime: A Dynamic Framework to Help Designers Keep Up with the Adaptive Criminal in a Changing World.' *International Journal of Risk, Security and Crime Prevention,* 2, 249-265.

HM Inspectorate of Constabulary (1998) Beating Crime. HMIC Thematic Inspection Report. London: Home Office.

Hope T., (1995) 'Community Crime Prevention.' In M. Tonry and D. P. Farrington (Eds). *Building a Safer Society: Strategic approaches to crime prevention.* Crime and Justice Vol 19. Chicago: University of Chicago Press.

Houghton G., (1992) *Car Theft in England and Wales: The Home Office Car Theft Index.* Crime Prevention Unit Paper 33. London: Home Office.

Levi M., P. Bissell and T. Richardson (1991) *The Prevention of Cheque and Credit Card Fraud.* Crime Prevention Paper 26. London: Home Office.

Levi M., and J. Handley (1998) *The Prevention of Plasic and Cheque Fraud Revisited.* Research Study 182. London: Home Office.

Mann D., and M. Sutton (1998) More change in the organization of thieving. *British Journal of Criminology,* 38, 201-229.

Matthews R., C.Pease and K.Pease (1998) 'Repeated Bank Robbery: Theme and Variations'. In G.Farrell and K.Pease (eds) *Research in Repeat Victimisation.* Monsey NY: Willow Tree Press (in press).

Platt C., (1997) 'Plotting Away in Margaritaville' *Wired* 5.7 140-179.

Roberts N.D., (1996) *Mobile Phone Crime.* Police Department: Home Office.

Rowlingson K., C. Whyley, T. Newburn and R. Bertoud (1997) 'Social security fraud: the role of penalties'. *Department of Social Security Research Report 64.* London: The Stationery Office.

Schwartz E.I., (1997) 'It's Not Retail' *Wired* 5.11 218-294.

Section II
Preventing crime in the community

5 Community crime prevention

Tim Hope

Introduction

Community crime prevention refers to actions intended to change the social conditions which sustain crime in residential communities (Hope, 1995). It concentrates on the ability of local social institutions to reduce crime. Local institutions bring people together within communities and, by doing so, transmit guidance and regulation of conduct and behaviour, especially to young people.

It is helpful to see approaches to community crime prevention operating in two, related, ways (Hope, 1995): first, along a 'horizontal dimension' of social relations amongst people and groups; and second, along a 'vertical' dimension of relations which connect local institutions to the wider community of civil society. Actions along both dimensions are necessary to implement effective crime prevention through the strengthening of social institutions.

Distribution of crime amongst communities

The chief justification for community-based crime prevention is that high rates of crime are a feature of certain residential communities (Bottoms and Wiles, 1997). This rationale for community-wide prevention measures derives from two sources:

i)   There is a community effect, which these high rates indicate, that could be due to factors which concentrate high-risk people in particular neighbourhoods, or to particular forms of community-relations, leading to high rates of local offending, victimisation and disorder; and,

ii) Alongside high rates of crime, these communities also have high rates of other social problems including poverty, income inequality and deprivation. The rationale for prevention stems either from a belief that common, causal reasons for crime and other social problems can be found in the social and material conditions of such communities, or that it is more efficient to target preventive measures in places which display multiple problems.

Community crime risks

Our most recent and reliable source about the nature of the distribution of community crime rates comes from the British Crime Survey, which measures the incidence of crime victimisation:

i) the community distribution of crime risk is very unequal. Over a half of all survey recorded property crimes, and over a third of all property crime victims, are likely to be found in just a fifth of the communities in England and Wales. Conversely, the least affected half of the country now experiences only 15 per cent of the crime, spread between a quarter of crime victims (Trickett et al, 1992; Hope, 1996; 1997); and,

ii) in addition to those factors which shape an individual or household's vulnerability to victimisation there is a risk which comes specifically from residence in communities with particular social characteristics (Osborn et al., 1996; Ellingworth et al, 1997; Osborn and Tseloni, 1995).

High crime areas

Broadly, research suggests that there are two kinds of high crime community in England and Wales:

i) *areas of concentrated poverty*, including council housing estates, characterised by a greater likelihood for poor, economically isolated and disadvantaged households to be living in close, residential proximity to those with similar disadvantages. Here, low skilled and otherwise disadvantaged youth often fail to gain access to the primary labour market. Such conditions bring together vulnerable victims and potential offenders; and,

ii) *pockets of social inequality* alongside multi-ethnic communities or relatively affluent urban enclaves also have high crime rates. Such inner urban areas are subject to rapid demographic change and transience, which may itself promote high crime rates, and which also bring the better- and worse-off into closest proximity, heightening inequalities between them and providing targets and motives for crime.

Concentration of problems

One of the distinctive features of the growth of crime and other problems in communities are concentration effects (Sampson and Wilson, 1995; Wilson, 1987) – the ways in which social difficulties can ratchet together and amplify each other into a spiral of deterioration. Various kinds of concentration effect seem to be occurring in high crime communities in Britain:

i) *compound social dislocations* - that is, an accumulation of social problems alongside crime, including drug-misuse, family violence, teenage pregnancy, children taken into care, and school failure;

ii) *criminal embeddedness of local youth* – that is, the greater likelihood that young people will become more deeply and persistently embedded in a criminal way of life (Hagan, 1994);

iii) *disorder* – residents of high crime communities also see their communities as having high levels of environmental disorder (including vandalism and graffiti), and disorderly conduct in public;

iv) *repeated, localised victimisation* – the rate of victimisation per victim in high crime areas is also much higher than that experienced by victims in lower crime areas (Trickett et al., 1992), resulting in disproportionately more repeat victimisation in high crime areas;

v) *diminishing informal control* – residents of high-crime areas find it hard to initiate and sustain voluntary activities without outside support, especially if these are oriented towards crime (Hope, 1995). Additionally, residents find it hard to muster sufficient resources to supervise the behaviour of young people, or to protect themselves from the behaviour of troublesome families; and,

vi) *criminal networks* – in some circumstances, forms of criminal organisation and networks can become established on high-crime estates. Though these are rarely of 'mafia' or gang-like sophistication, they nevertheless sustain illicit activities and markets which can fuel crime.

Safe neighbourhoods

Broadly, as high-rates of crime are associated with the concentration of poverty so, conversely, low crime rates are associated with the concentration of affluent households in an area (Ellingworth et al. 1997; Osborn and Tseloni, 1995; Hirschfield and Brown, 1997). The very unequal distribution in crime risk between communities means that many communities have very much lower rates of crime than the high crime ones. Yet residents of some of these communities worry, nevertheless, about crime and disorder – worries which are bound-up with other anxieties about their communities. That this 'fear' of crime has only a partial basis in the actual risk of victimisation does not inhibit such communities from calling for greater police protection and crime prevention support.

The delivery of crime prevention to communities

Over the past 15 years, many countries have begun to develop national and local machinery for organising and delivering crime prevention to local communities. In general, there seems to be a consensus that community crime prevention is delivered most effectively through inter-agency co-ordination at the local level. Nevertheless, structures and arrangements vary in different ways from country to country, including whether:

- the focus is specifically upon crime prevention or on broader issues such as 'social exclusion' (e.g. France) or 'community safety' (Italy, Spain);

- there is a single dominant or lead agency such as the police (e.g., US) or shared responsibilities amongst agencies (e.g., Britain);

- arrangements for community safety are part of the democratic process of local government led by municipalities (e.g., France, Italy, The Netherlands) or have involved 'partnership' arrangements between agencies both within and outside local government (e.g., Britain, Canada, Australia);

- the delivery of crime prevention is governed by statutory, legal or 'contractual' powers and duties – involving both agencies and citizens – or whether such arrangements are mounted on an informal or voluntary basis;

- there is a consistency of approach (France) or variation (Britain, Germany) between localities;

- substantial, new resources have been provided (France, The Netherlands); or,

- there has been central government leadership in approach (France), servicing and support (Britain, Sweden, The Netherlands), or whether support has come sub-nationally – e.g. at federal state (US, Germany), regional (Italy) or city level (US).

This variety of arrangements around the basic consensus of multi-agency co-ordination is a reflection both of different nations' cultures and traditions of governance, and different political philosophies about crime, safety, exclusion and policing. There has been some research comparing approaches adopted between Britain, France (Pitts and Hope, 1997; King 1991) and Germany (Lacey and Zedner, 1997). This research has tended to focus on the origins and nature of the different practices adopted rather than on a comparative evaluation of their effectiveness in reducing crime; the question as to which set of arrangements would reduce crime and disorder most effectively has not been addressed specifically, and would be difficult to answer scientifically.

There has also been variation amongst local partnership approaches in Britain, which may reflect different local arrangements and relationships between agencies (Home Office, 1991; Liddle and Gelsthorpe, 1994a, b, c). These initiatives usually consist of project or programme-level management arrangements whose remit may cover a wider area, and specific prevention schemes – often staffed by local professionals – usually targeted at smaller areas such as city centres or particular residential areas or estates. National coverage of partnership arrangements is patchy and variable, and schemes are of relatively short duration. Levels of funding of schemes have been modest and time-limited, with 'new' funding coming more often from targeted programmes (SRB, Safer Cities) than from reallocation of main spending programmes.

There has been case-study research into local examples of multi-agency crime prevention. Where difficulties and problems of implementation have been encountered, their origins can be found in part in the structures and processes of local governance in Britain, including: endemic difficulties in providing co-ordinated services to specific targeted groups (Audit Commission, 1996); relations between criminal justice and local authority agencies; and 'quasi-market' regimes for managing performance and efficiency, which make co-ordinated crime prevention a 'costly' option for local agencies (Pitts and Hope, 1997). A general problem is that difficulties of co-ordination and implementation can lead to waste, inefficiency and lack of effectiveness in the local delivery of crime prevention.

The provisions of the forthcoming Crime and Disorder Bill will change some of these circumstances by providing statutory clarification of some of these responsibilities and duties. Likewise, the joint duty upon the police and local authorities to devise and monitor community safety plans for their districts may provide an overarching framework for local action. There is a need, however, for evaluative research to monitor the impact of the new provisions on the delivery of crime prevention to local communities. There is also a need to monitor how the new arrangements for delivery of community safety mesh with other local plans for delivering benefits and services to high crime communities, both in the field of criminal justice (e.g., policing plans), social services (e.g., children's services), and other cross-cutting programmes of social policy – especially the New Deal.

Local programmes

There are now a number of descriptions of community-oriented or community-based programmes (e.g., Bright, 1997; Utting, 1996; Bennett and Graham, 1995; Osborn and Shaftoe, 1995; Safe Neighbourhoods Unit, 1993); and a number of ways in which they might be classified (see Hope, 1995, Bennett and Graham, 1995). Space precludes a detailed gazette of programmes and schemes.

Types of programme

Community-focused prevention programmes might be classified as:

i) *community-organisation* – typically, these build community-based associations, and linkages to local schools, churches, etc. – which can then provide effective socialisation for young people, including local adults as positive role models (Hope, 1995);

ii) *community defence* – these approaches are aimed at preventing victimisation by deterring offending by those who do not belong to the community. They include strategies of crime prevention through environmental design (CPTED), defensible space measures, and the intentional organising of community surveillance through Neighbourhood Watch;

iii) *order-maintenance* – in part embodying the theory of 'broken windows' – and also called 'zero tolerance' – these approaches seek to control both physical disorder (litter, vandalism, graffiti), threatening neighbours and rowdy street behaviour;

iv) *risk-based programmes* – these relatively recent approaches seek to identify risk factors amongst community populations, to identify those most at risk, and to deliver preventive resources specifically for them. Their rationale is that community change can be brought about by changing individuals rather than vice versa (as has often been the case with earlier interventions). They include approaches targeted on victimisation, e.g., strategies aimed at the protection of victims and the prevention of repeat victimisation – and those aimed at the development of offending amongst local young people, e.g., the Communities that Care Programme (CTC, 1997);

v) *community development* – these strategies seek to rebuild the social, physical and economic fabric of neighbourhoods and include:

(a) improvements to the built environment;

(b) decentralised housing management and services;

(c) changes in the social mix through housing allocation policies;

(d) policies which lead to the social and economic regeneration of neighbourhoods (Bennett and Graham, 1995); and,

vi) *structural change* – while similar in aim to 'community development' (v. above), these 'strategies' see the main changes in communities – with the greatest consequences for crime reduction – as stemming primarily from the operation of more macro-level policies in economic development and employment, housing markets, education, health provision, and the delivery of welfare, benefits and other social services. In this view, much of the space for action against community-level social dislocation (including crime) depends upon the interaction of social policies – which although experienced locally may not be amenable to change at the local level.

In practice, actual programmes rarely conform consistently to one or the other models described above. Most programmes often resemble 'comprehensive community initiatives' (CCIs) – programmes consisting of a mixture of measures and implementation strategies which aim to bring about change holistically in local areas (Connell, et al., 1995).

Evaluation

There are major methodological and practical difficulties in evaluating the effectiveness of community-based prevention programmes and very few crime prevention CCIs have been evaluated with any great degree of scientific rigour.

Effectiveness

While it is possible to assemble relevant evidence and promising examples of good practice (Crime Prevention Digest, 1997; Crime Concern, 1996) –

which may be regarded as an adequate basis for policy making – clear, general and scientifically reliable statements about 'what works' in community crime prevention cannot yet be made. Some considerations arising from research which may affect implementation and effectiveness can be listed, briefly:

i) *informal social control* – measures which rely exclusively on the voluntary actions of local residents to exert control over the behaviour of co-residents or non-residents are unlikely to be successful (Hope, 1995);

ii) *fragility* – the efficacy of local actions to bring about community change (such as efforts to increase estate stability and reduce disorder) can be undermined by more powerful, exogenous factors (such as external economic pressures);

iii) *quantity and mix of measures* – although we know that single-focus measures are less likely to bring about community change in crime rates than multiple measures (Osborn and Shaftoe, 1995) we know less about the most effective kinds of 'mix' of measures;

iv) *scale of the intervention (dosage)* – we suspect that

  (a) larger changes can be achieved more often in smaller areas;

  (b) more expenditure of preventive effort can yield more return in crime reduction (Ekblom, 1997); and,

v) *institutional infrastructure* - the 'vertical' dimension of a neighbourhood's relations with the wider community is equally important for implementing change to reduce crime. Residents of communities with a weak infrastructure of institutions (paragraph 1), or where institutions and agencies are working at cross-purposes, have to take the burden of social control upon their own shoulders.

Conclusion

The research evidence assembled suggests that community crime prevention initiatives are most likely to be successful if strategies are used that:

i) target crime prevention efforts on high crime communities; and

ii) apply comprehensive community initiatives to tackle the interlocking problems of social dislocation, of which crime plays an important part.

Nevertheless, while there are a variety of programme ideas, many of which have been applied in practice, the problems of evaluation and the paucity of reliable (scientific) evaluations provide a weak evidential base upon which to assess cost-effectiveness. In deciding upon whether and how best to deliver effective crime prevention, policy-makers will need to make strategic decisions chiefly about the costs of *not* intervening to address the complexity of social dislocation in high crime communities.

References

Audit Commission (1996) *Misspent Youth...young people and crime.* London: Audit Commission for Local Authorities and the National Health Service in England and Wales.

Bennett, T., and J. Graham (1995) *Crime Prevention Strategies in Europe and North America.* Helsinki: HEUNI.

Bottoms, A.E., and P. Wiles (1997). 'Environmental criminology'. In Maguire, M., R. Morgan and R. Reiner (Eds.) *The Oxford Handbook of Criminology: second edition* Oxford: Clarendon Press.

Bright, J., (1997) *Turning the tide: crime, community and prevention.* London: Demos.

Connell, J. P., et al. (1995) *New Approaches to Evaluating Community Initiatives.* Washington, DC: The Aspen Institute.

Communities that Care (UK). (1997) *Communities that Care.* York: Joseph Rowntree Foundation.

Crime Concern (1996) *Reducing Crime and Criminality in High Crime Neighbourhoods.* Briefing Paper No. 3. Swindon: Crime Concern.

Crime Prevention Digest (1997) Montreal: International Centre for the Prevention of Crime.

Ekblom, P., (1997) 'Gearing up against Crime: A Dynamic Framework to Help Designers Keep up with the Adaptive Criminal in a Changing World.' *International Journal of Risk, Security and Crime Prevention,* 2, 249-265.

Ellingworth, D., T. Hope, D. R. Osborn, A. Trickett and K. Pease (1997) 'Prior victimisation and crime risk' *International Journal of Risk, Security and Crime Prevention,* 2, 201-214.

Hagan, J., (1994). *Crime and Disrepute.* Thousand Oaks, CA: Pine Forge Press.

Hirschfield, A.F.G., and P. J. Brown (1997) *Crime and the spatial Concentration of Disadvantage: an analysis for Merseyside.* Crime and Social Order Programme, Economic and Social Research Council: End of Award Report (summary available at http://www.salford.ac.uk/isr/cover.htm)

Home Office (1991). *Safer Communities: the local delivery of crime prevention through the partnership approach.* Report of a Working Group (James Morgan, Chair). Standing Conference on Crime Prevention. London: Home Office.

Hope, T., (1995). 'Community Crime Prevention'. In M. Tonry and D.P. Farrington (Eds.). *Building a Safer Society: strategic approaches to crime prevention.* Crime and Justice, vol. 19. Chicago: University of Chicago Press.

Hope, T., (1996). 'Communities, crime and inequality in England and Wales.' In T. Bennett (Ed.) *Preventing Crime and Disorder: targeting strategies and responsibilities.* Cambridge: Institute of Criminology.

Hope T., (1997) Inequality and the Future of Community Crime Prevention in Lab, S. P. (Ed.) *Crime Prevention at a Crossroads.* American Academy of Criminal Justice Sciences Monograph Series, Cincinnati, OH, Anderson Publishing.

King M., (1991). 'The political construction of crime prevention: a contrast between the French and British experience'. In Stenson, K. and D. Cowell (Eds). *The Politics of Crime Control.* London: Sage.

Lacey, N., and L. Zedner (1997) Social Order, Criminal Justice and the Appeal to Community in Britain and Germany. Crime and Social Order Programme, Economic and Social Research Council: End of Award Report (summary available at http://www.salford.ac.uk/isr/cover.htm).

Liddle, A.M., and L.R. Gelsthorpe (1994a) *Inter-Agency Crime Prevention: Organizing Local Delivery.* Paper No. 52, Police Research Group, Crime Prevention Unit Series. London: Home Office Police Department.

Liddle, A.M., and L.R. Gelsthorpe (1994b) *Crime Prevention and Inter-Agency Co-operation.* Paper No. 53, Police Research Group, Crime Prevention Unit Series. London: Home Office Police Department.

Liddle, A.M., and L.R. Gelsthorpe (1994c) *Inter-Agency Crime Prevention: Further Issues.* Supplementary Paper to CPU Series Paper No. 52 and 53, Police Research Group, Crime Prevention Unit Series. London: Home Office Police Department.

Osborn, D.R., and A. Tseloni (1995). The Distribution of Household Property Crimes. The University of Manchester School of Economic Studies Discussion Paper No. 9530. Manchester: University of Manchester (and forthcoming in the *Journal of Quantitative Criminology*).

Osborn, D.R., D. Ellingworth, T. Hope, and A. Trickett (1996). Are repeatedly victimized households different? *Journal of Quantitative Criminology,* 12, 223-245.

Osborn, S., and H. Shaftoe (1995) *Safe Neighbourhoods?* London: Safe Neighbourhoods Unit.

Pitts, J., and T. Hope (1997) 'The local politics of inclusion: the state and community safety'. *Social Policy and Administration,* 31, 37-58.

Safe Neighbourhoods Unit (1993). *Crime Prevention on Council Estates.* Department of the Environment. London: HMSO.

Sampson, R.J., and Wilson, W.J., (1995) 'Toward a theory of race, crime and urban inequality'. In Hagan, J. and Peterson, R.D. (Eds) *Crime and Inequality.* Stanford, CA: Stanford University Press.

Trickett, A., D. R. Osborn, J. Seymour and K. Pease (1992) "What is different about high crime areas?" *British Journal of Criminology,* 32: 81-89.

Utting, D., (1996) *Reducing Criminality Among Young People.* Home Office Research Study 161. London: Home Office.

Wilson W. J., (1987) *The Truly Disadvantaged: the Inner City, the Underclass and Public Policy,* Chicago, University of Chicago Press.

6 Effective policing strategies for reducing crime

Peter Jordan

Introduction

The purpose of this chapter is to summarise the research about the relative effectiveness of different police strategies, tactics or practices in reducing crime. There are three preliminary remarks to be made. The first is a cautionary aside; the second is a general point about the importance of enthusiastic implementation; and the third is a more substantive issue to do with what research evidence is available in this country and in the US.

Cautionary comments

First, the tight focus of this section upon the police objective of *'reducing criminality and the opportunities for crime, and promoting social responsibility'* means that it pays little regard to other police objectives such as maintenance of order and catching perpetrators. A consistent finding of police research is that policing is very complex and there are subtle consequences of any action the police take which may not be immediately apparent. If the debate moves on to consider these potential trade-offs, some framework for mapping and discussing such interactions will be required.

Enthusiastic implementation

Second, although there are some strategies which research indicates are not generally effective, there are always instances in which those strategies do work. These tend to be distinguished by the vigour and enthusiasm with which they are pursued, and the degree to which they are well matched to the problem they are addressing. While not dismissing that experience, this section looks for strategies which are less dependent upon high calibre personnel.

Research

Two broad research approaches can be distinguished. The first can be summarised as randomised allocation of some strategy to a range of areas; the second, as in-depth study of a strategy in a small number of areas. The former will show in broad terms *whether* something works; the latter offers some hope of understanding *how* and *why* an intervention works and of tuning it to exert maximum effect in whatever practical circumstances it is applied.

The first approach is used more in the US and, provided it covers a wide range of area types, offers a realistic hope of saying that something that works in specific social contexts is 'generalizable to similar settings in other places and times' (Sherman et al., 1997). UK research has tended to favour the second approach rather than the first. This has generated principles relating to the context and mechanisms by which results are achieved (Pawson and Tilley, 1997).

Research findings are rarely unequivocal. Individual studies can always be criticised by other professionals, and indeed, usually are. This makes it hard to draw any definite lessons for future action. The current paper draws heavily on the work of Sherman whose chapter in the report to the US Congress (Sherman et al., 1997) is the only available work which pulls together the results of many formal, statistically based evaluations of police initiatives aimed at reducing crime. In an attempt to draw unequivocal lessons from research, he sorts the initiatives into categories; provides a method of ranking studies by the rigour of their methodology; and, adopts a stringent criterion for declaring a strategy a success. A fuller description of the criteria is given in Annex A.

If we were to accept that criterion strictly, it would exclude much UK research which throws a slightly different, and useful, light on the issue of 'what works'. Fortunately, he does allow that if many studies seem to point to the same conclusion, then their collective results should be accepted at least as a strong indication that the strategy in question is worth pursuing. This admits the UK research on a number of topics, but more important than that is the broad conclusion of the UK work which is that the police have to adopt a locally relevant tactic within a strategic framework and implement it with sensitivity to the problem being addressed and to the local conditions. This calls for local crime audits, good intelligence systems, proper strategic management, monitoring of performance, responsiveness to the constantly changing crime picture, and creativity. Despite the paucity of statistical evidence, in Sherman's terms, that these things contribute to reducing crime, those who have been closest to the UK trials have a strong sense that they most certainly do so.

Structure of this chapter

The presentation of research findings in this chapter is structured around a categorisation of police strategies for combating crime. Evidence is presented on which of these strategies work; which do not; which look promising and therefore worth further investigation; and which issues have not been studied sufficiently to draw any conclusion. Finally it looks at what needs to be done to fill the gaps both in the form of formal evaluation exercises and in the development of routine police performance measures which can be used to monitor the effectiveness of their work.

Categorisation of police strategies for preventing crime

The table below, adapted from Sherman et al., (1997) categorises the strategies by which the police may seek to play a significant role in reducing crime. These range from the naive 'more police means less crime' to the more sophisticated 'problem oriented policing'. Each strategy is accompanied by a one line summary of the underlying hypothesis, and the indications of research. The following paragraphs enlarge a little on the research findings.

Table 6.1 Possible police strategies for reducing crime

Strategy	Underlying hypothesis	Summary of research indications about the underlying hypothesis
1. Increase the numbers of police.	The more police a city employs, the less crime it will have.	Effect of overall numbers is unclear.
2. Random Patrol.	The more random patrol a city receives, the more a perceived "omnipresence" of the police will deter crime in public places.	Not effective.
3. Increase the use of the police power of arrest.	The more arrests police make in response to reported or observed offences of any kind, the less crime there will be.	Effective in some domestic violence situations: counterproductive for juveniles.
4. Contact with the community in general.	The greater quantity and better quality of contacts between police and citizens, the less crime.	Not generally effective except where the objective is to increase police 'legitimacy' with the public.
5. Informal contact with children.	Informal contact between police and young people will dissuade those likely to offend from doing so.	Not generally effective.

Table 6.1 Possible police strategies for reducing crime (cont'd)

6. Respond quickly to emergency calls.	The shorter the police travel time from assignment to arrival at a crime scene, the less crime there will be.	Mixed evidence. US research finds it ineffective, but indications from UK work are that it may yield a marginal improvement in clear ups for burglary.
7. Target high profile crimes or criminals.	The higher the police-initiated arrest rate for high-risk offenders and offences, the lower the rates of serious or violent crime.	Targeting repeat offenders appears to be worthwhile, but targeting drug markets is less effective.
8. Directed patrol.	The more precisely patrol presence is concentrated at the "hot spots" and "hot times" of criminal activity, the less crime there will be in those places and times.	US evidence is that this is an effective strategy for dealing with local problems.
9. Targeting repeat victims.	Crime can be reduced by protecting victims from further crime.	UK research indicates that this can effect a significant reduction in certain types of crime.
10. Inter-agency working.	The police can prevent crime by working in partnership with, or providing crime related information to, other agencies, mainly Local Authorities but, with the intention of informing the national effort to reduce crime, perhaps also the DETR, DfEE, Probation Service etc.	UK evidence is that this can be a very useful mode of working for the police.
11 Problem-Oriented Policing.	If police can identify specific patterns of crime and analyse the underlying problems in the community, they are more likely to come up with solutions that reduce the number of criminal incidents.	The main tenet of this rational approach has been tested on a small scale, but formal evaluation of the impact on crime in a wider implementation is awaited.

What doesn't work

The conclusion of Sherman's survey is that, using the criteria of consistent findings from two methodologically sound studies (at least level three of his scale), some strategies can be judged effective and others ineffective. However, there is some contrary evidence from UK research which does not fit into Sherman's framework but should certainly not be ignored.

Random patrol

The research evidence seems to be fairly clear that random patrol does not have a marked effect upon crime levels (Press, 1971; Kelling et al, 1974; Larson, 1975; Fienberg et al.,1976; Farrington, 1977; Police Foundation, 1981; Trojanowicz, 1986; Felson, 1994). It may, of course, have other objectives.

Charging more suspects

i)   As a general policy

The US evidence (Tittle and Rowe, 1974; Logan, 1975; Brown, 1978; Greenberg et al., 1979; Greenberg and Kessler, 1982; Chamlin,1988, 1991) points to the conclusion that, as a general policy, higher charging rates per crime do not have any noticeable effect on crime levels. However there are specific situations in which increased use of charging may be effective and others where it is counter-productive. For example, for juveniles higher charge rates may ultimately lead to higher levels of offending (see below).

ii)   Legalistic processing of juveniles for minor offences

The conclusions in this area rest mainly on one rigorous, randomised exercise in the US (Gold and Williams, 1970), in which the personal characteristics and offences of the 'charged' and 'not charged' groups were matched. Here 'charging' refers to the process of putting juveniles through the full legal process, culminating in trial. The study found that those 'charged' were more likely to reoffend. The effect was particularly strong if the processing was highly 'legalistic'.

A number of less rigorous studies (Klein, 1986; Smith and Gartin, 1989; Huizinga and Esbensen, 1992) point to the same conclusion (although one study found that first offenders were less likely to reoffend if they were formally charged with their first offence, but did confirm that others were more likely to reoffend if charged than if not). These findings suggest that some implementations of low tolerance policing may be counterproductive in the medium term. Note that the research does not suggest ignoring minor offences. It merely reinforces the view already prevalent in the UK, that cautioning is a more effective alternative to charging during the early stages of offending.

Community policing

Maintenance of good community relations is clearly important but the attempts by the police, detailed below, to become closer to the public and involve them in addressing policing problems have been shown to be less successful than others described later.

i)   Neighbourhood watch

Neighbourhood Watch schemes have been implemented in widely differing contexts, but most commonly in areas of relative affluence and low crime rates. Areas with very high crime rates pose particular problems in introducing and maintaining schemes (Laycock and Tilley, 1995). Thus, although there is evidence that schemes can, in certain circumstances, reduce crime (particularly burglary), it is unlikely that existing implementations have had a marked effect in preventing crime nationally. Whatever the reasons, the research suggests that the mere establishment of neighbourhood watch schemes cannot be expected to bring down crime automatically (Lindsay and McGillis,1986; Rosenbaum et al., 1986; Pate et al., 1987; Bennett, 1990). To be successful, they need to be planned and introduced with sensitivity to community dynamics (Laycock and Tilley, 1995).

ii)   Community policing without clear focus

Other work suggests that community policing initiatives aimed solely at increasing the quantity and quality of police-citizen contacts are not generally very effective (Wycoff et al.,1985; Wycoff and Skogan, 1986; Skogan et al., 1995: Sherman et al., 1995). The specific studies reported cover attempts to increase the flow of information about local crime from the police to the public and opening 'police shops' to make it easier and less daunting to contact the police.

Drug market arrests

This refers to the strategy of disrupting drug-related business in areas and houses where drug dealing takes place. The idea being that drugs and other crime go together so removing the drugs will remove other crime, particularly violence. The research evidence is that this does not happen, at least in the American context, though in some cases there have been some short term (7-12 days) reductions in robbery and other crimes (Kleiman,

1988; Zimmer, 1990; Uchida et al., 1992; Sviridoff, et al., 1992; Annan and Skogan, 1993; Sherman and Rogan 1995; Weisburd and Green, 1995). No hypothesis is offered for any connection between drug dealing and violence so it is difficult to guess whether this result is transferable to the British context. There may, of course be other reasons for harassing drug dealers in order specifically to disrupt the local drug markets.

On this last point, there has been some UK research on tackling local drug markets (reviewed in Hough (1996). Research by Edmunds et.al., (1996) concentrated on the mechanics of the markets, the kinds of people who used them etc. It did not evaluate specific prevention strategies and concluded that:

> "The body of knowledge about effective action against drug markets remains scanty.........it is simply not possible to offer a more prescriptive set of solutions to the police service and their partner agencies. *The best mix of tactics will vary widely according to local circumstances*." (our italics).

Proactive work with children

There has been one rigorous study of this approach to crime prevention in the UK (Heal and Laycock, 1987). The Staffordshire police's SPACE scheme covered about 25,000 children over the summer holidays. It took up a lot of police effort and showed no effect on crime when compared to neighbouring forces.

Increasing fast response

The evidence for this strategy is conflicting (Isaacs, 1967; Holliday, 1974; Brown, 1974; Pate et al., 1976; Kansas City Police Department, 1977; Clawson and Chang, 1977; Chaiken, 1978; Goldstein,1979; Spelman and Brown, 1981). Indirect US evidence is that it is of no value in reducing crime not least because calls from the public tend to be made some time after the incident has occurred. There may, of course be other reasons, e.g. public reassurance, for providing a rapid response service.

Current UK research (Coupe and Griffiths, 1996), based on an examination of the methods employed in the normal course of events to clear up domestic burglaries in the West Midlands, is more positive. The researchers observed that 10 per cent of burglaries were reported while still in progress and that more of these burglars were caught when the response was faster. They calculated that faster response overall would enable the police to catch more burglars in the act. The estimate made was that by investing (a great deal) more police effort in rapid response, it might be possible to increase clear-ups from six per cent to eight per cent. The proposals arising from this work are being evaluated.

Effective strategies

Using Sherman's criterion, the strategies listed in the box below have been shown to be *effective* in reducing crime:

Effective strategies
 • **targeting repeat offenders;** • **targeting repeat victims;** • **police patrols directed at 'hot-spots'; and,** • **targeting drink driving.**

Targeting repeat offenders

There is clear evidence that targeting high rate offenders, and high risk places and times can be successful in achieving its aims (Martin and Sherman, 1986; Abrahamse et al., 1991), although targeting drug dealing locations appears – from American experience – to be an exception to this rule. The exercises which targeted individuals were aimed at securing sound evidence, convictions and long sentences and they were successful in their aims. Any impact on crime prevention would have been through incapacitation of the offenders and, possibly, through deterring other criminals, but these effects were not evaluated.

Targeting repeat victims

UK research has paid a lot of attention to the observation that some victims suffer a disproportionate amount of crime (Tilley, 1993; Chenery et al., 1997). This suggests a way for the police to prevent crime pro-actively. Several research projects, looking at strategies based on this approach in different contexts and for different offences, indicate that it can be very effective in reducing the incidence of repeat victimisation and have a significant impact on overall crime levels. The Kirkholt and Huddersfield exercises showed quite large reductions in domestic burglary. In both cases, the role of partnership work between police and local authorities was an important element in their success.

Directed patrol

The US evidence here is quite strong and consistent (Cohen and Felson 1979; Buerger et al., 1995; Koper, 1995). Certain categories of crime are susceptible to the visible presence of police officers, and patrols directed at places and times where those crimes are known to occur ('hot-spots') will prevent the occurrence of crime (even when account is taken of displacement effects). The studies found evidence that the time for the police to be at the hot-spot, which maximised their effect, was around 15 minutes.

The increased level of police presence in some of these studies was quite large. The figures quoted vary from 40 per cent – 400 per cent more police presence at the hot-spots. Others simply describe the increased presence as 'saturation patrols'. This increased presence cut crime by up to 50 per cent in some cases. However the resonance of the term 'saturation policing' is obvious and suggests that the strategy would need to be used with care to avoid provoking negative reactions in the community.

Targeting drink driving

Strategies to reduce drink driving provide clear success stories in a wide range of countries including Britain (Ross, 1973; Boydstun, 1975; Ross, 1975; Ross, 1977; Hurst, and Wright, 1980; Ross, 1981; Ross et al., 1982). Initial reductions were achieved by increasing the risk of being caught and the severity of punishment, but subsequently there has been a change in public attitudes to the activity and understanding of the dangers it poses. The mix of strategies required need not be dwelt on further here.

Strategies worth a closer look

The evidence suggests that the strategies shown in the box below may have value, but is not clear enough at present to give them a definite recommendation.

Strategies worth further study

- community participation in priority setting;
- improving police legitimacy with the community;
- domestic violence strategies;
- order maintenance (but avoiding damage to legitimacy); and,
- problem oriented policing.

Community participation in priority setting

Research on this approach to involving the community is not sufficiently rigorous to endorse it, but experience reported from Chicago suggests that it is capable of involving citizens in high crime areas in a way that neighbourhood watch fails to do although there is no evidence yet as to its impact on crime levels (Wycoff and Skogan,1993).

Improving police legitimacy with the community

The concept of legitimacy corresponds to the British concept of policing by consent. The research finding is that effort put into reducing fear and suspicion of the police, and treating people (including offenders) with respect has (a) a positive effect on the degree of co-operation the police get from the community; (b) it lowers the '*perceived* serious crime level' and (c) it reduces recidivism for domestic violence (Tyler, 1990; Skogan, 1990; Skogan et al., 1995; Paternoster et al., 1996).

Included under this heading is the use of 'community accountability conferences' (in British terms – restorative justice) in which the offender and victim meet and some agreement is reached to repay the cost of the crime to the victim – failure to do so on the part of the offender results in prosecution. Preliminary findings show that, regardless of the outcome, this procedure results in greater respect for the police and 'justice'. The impact on crime levels is unclear.

Domestic violence strategies

US experience of arresting suspects for domestic assaults appear to suggest that the results achievable are context-dependent. It works better when suspects have strong social ties and worse when they have nothing to lose. Where suspects were in employment, the experience of arrest appeared to reduce the risk of repeat offending (Sherman and Berk, 1984; Hirschel et al., 1990), while offending was repeated when unemployed perpetrators were arrested (Sherman and Berk, 1984; Hirschel et al., 1990; Dunford, 1990; Dunford et al., 1990; Sherman et al., 1991; Pate et al., 1991; Pate and Hamilton, 1992; Dunford, 1992; Berk et al., 1992a; Berk et al.,1992b; Marciniak, 1994). However, there is some doubt about how to interpret these measurements. It is hard to decide whether the findings are applicable to Britain, where the context of domestic violence and unemployment may both be very different.

Order maintenance

'Order maintenance' is taken here to mean concentrating police effort on a small area with particular crime problems, and policing it very strictly. It is not to be understood as a police strategy for universal application within a force. It has sometimes been called 'zero tolerance'. Research suggests that it must be used with caution (Schwartz and Skolnick, 1962; Pate and Skogan, 1985; Reiss, 1985; Sherman, 1990; Kelling and Coles, 1996; Bushway, 1996). There is moderately strong evidence that it can reduce serious crime in the short term, but there are large question marks over the ability of the police to distinguish between firm and harsh policing styles, and over the long term effect of arresting many more people for relatively minor offences. Police tactics in some implementations of zero-tolerance have been described as over-zealous and this can lead to poor police-community relations (Scarman, 1981).

The long term impact of increasing arrests for minor offences may be to damage police legitimacy and to increase the number of people with criminal records and consequent difficulty finding work. What data there are suggest that zero-tolerance may offer an attractive short term reduction in crime, but that it must also be evaluated against its long term effects on those arrested, and the communities from which they come.

Problem oriented policing (POP)

The idea behind POP is very simple (Leigh et al., 1996). It suggests that policing should be about solving the underlying problems in the community that come to the attention of the police – not simply responding to calls. Goldstein, who first advocated POP in 1979, has argued that to do this a service must be oriented to creating the conditions and providing the resources to allow problem solving to take place routinely (Goldstein, 1979, 1990). Officers must know the underlying issues locally, be in contact with the community; have information to help understand the nature of the underlying problems that generate clusters of incidents; be supported by senior officers in attempting to solve problems imaginatively and tailor problem-solving to emerging local issues.

This is a demanding agenda that can be seen as threatening. Not surprisingly, where POP has been attempted it has generally been in a very diluted form. Many police services in North America claim to use it. Leigh et al. (1996) summarise some of the attempts to introduce strategies labelled as POP to England and Wales. They conclude that most were based on relatively small-scale, "ring-fenced teams" operating in a conventional management environment, with no formal assessment of outcomes. Some recent implementations have attempted to follow Goldstein's model more closely. Formal evaluation of these have yet to be published.

Some of the strategies described earlier in this chapter (such as directed patrol and targeting repeat offenders) are approaches that can result from POP in specific contexts.

Conclusions

The research literature shows that in certain circumstances, the police have made a significant impact upon *local* crime rates. In general, success follows on selection of the appropriate tactic for the problem under attack; effective management and good targeting of resources. Depending on the particular approach adopted, the police may be acting alone (e.g. targeted patrol), or in partnership with others (e.g. targeting repeat victims). The UK research also shows, however, that there is room for improvement in their capacity to capture relevant data, and put it to effective use; in their management techniques; and in their willingness to adopt good practice. These issues are currently being addressed. Assuming these issues are resolved, the great question becomes, can the local reductions in crime which we believe the police can achieve, be replicated in sufficient number to have a noticeable effect on national crime rates?

Future of evaluation

Where there is still uncertainty about particular police strategies there is obvious need for rigorous evaluations that would include a series of studies to refine our understanding of 'what works, for whom and in what circumstances'. This will be expensive, but research so far indicates that a lot of effort goes into ineffective practices and the saving arising from research could be much larger than its cost. The current drive to develop better routine performance measures for police also provides an opportunity to distinguish effective working practices more systematically. A package of police performance measures could be used to discriminate police management units at all levels, from force to beat, and relate the outcomes achieved more rigorously to styles and strategies.

References

Abrahamse, A.F., P.A. Ebener, P.W. Greenwood, N.Fitzgerald, and T. E. Kosin (1991). An Experimental Evaluation of the Phoenix Repeat Offender Program. *Justice Quarterly* 8:141-168.

Annan, S., and W. Skogan (1993). *Drug Enforcement in Public Housing: Signs of Success in Denver.* Washington, DC: Police Foundation.

Bennett, T., (1990). *Evaluating Neighbourhood Watch.* Basingstoke: Gower.

Berk, R. A., A. Campbell, R. Klap, and B. Western (1992a). A Bayesian Analysis of the Colorado Spouse Abuse Experiment. *Journal of Criminal Law and Criminology* 83: 170-200.

Berk, R. A., A. Campbell, R. Klap, and B. Western (1992b) The Deterrent Effect of Arrest in Incidents of Domestic Violence: A Bayesian Analysis of Four Field Experiments. *American Sociological Review* 57: 698-708.

Boydstun, J., (1975). *The San Diego Field Interrogation Experiment.* Washington, DC: Police Foundation.

Brown, D. W., (1978). Arrests and Crime Rates: When Does a Tipping Effect Occur?. *Social Forces* 57: 671-82.

Brown, W., (1974). *Evaluation of Police Patrol Operations.* Unpublished MA Thesis, University of Ottowa.

Buerger, M. E., A. Petrosino and E. G. Cohn (1995). In J. Eck and D. Weisburd, eds. *Crime and Place.* Monsey, N.Y.: Criminal Justice Press and Police Executive Research Forum.

Bushway, S., (1996). *The Impact of a Criminal History Record on Access to Legitimate Employment.* PhD Dissertation, H. John. Heinz School of Public Policy and Management, Carnegie Mellon University.

Chaiken, J. M., (1978). What Is Known About Deterrent Effects of Police Activities. In James A. Cramer, ed., *Preventing Crime.* Beverly Hills, CA: Sage Publications.

Chamlin, M., (1988). Crimes and Arrest: An Autoregressive Integrated Moving Average (ARIMA) Approach. *Journal of Quantitative Criminology.*

Chamlin M., (1991). A Longitudinal Analysis of the Arrest-Crime Relationship: A further examination of the Tipping Effect. *Justice Quarterly,* 8, 187-199.

Chenery S., J. Holt and K. Pease (1997). B*iting Back II: Reducing Repeat Victimisation in Huddersfield.* Police Research Group CDPS Paper 82. London: Home Office.

Clawson, C., and S.K. Chang (1977). The Relationship of Response Delays and Arrest Rates. *Journal of Police Science and Administration.* 5: 53-68.

Cohen, L., and M. Felson (1979). Social Change and Crime Rate Trends: A Routine Activities Approach. *American Sociological Review* 44: 588-607.

Coupe T., and M. Griffiths (1996). *Solving Residential Burglary.* Police Research Group CDPS Paper 77. London: Home Office

Dunford, F. W., (1990). System-Initiated Warrants for Suspects of Misdemeanor Domestic Assault: A Pilot Study. *Justice Quarterly* 7: 631-653.

Dunford, F. W., (1992). The Measurement of Recidivism in Cases of Spouse Assault. *Journal of Criminal Law and Criminology* 83: 120-136.

Dunford, F. W., D. Huizinga, and D. S. Elliott (1990). The Role of Arrest in Domestic Assault: The Omaha Police Experiment. *Criminology* 28: 183-206.

Edmunds M., M. Hough and N. Urquia (1996). *Tackling Local Drug Markets.* Police Research Group CDPS Paper 80. London: Home Office.

Farrington, D. P., (1977). The Effects of Public Labelling. *British Journal of Criminology* 17: 112-25.

Felson, M., (1994). *Crime and Everyday Life.* Thousand Oaks, CA: Pine Forge Press.

Fienberg, S. E., K. Larntz, and A. J. Reiss, Jr. (1976). Redesigning the Kansas City Preventive Patrol Experiment. *Evaluation* 3: 124-131.

Gold, M., and J. Williams (1970). National Study of the Aftermath of Apprehension. *Prospectus* 3: 3-12.

Goldstein, H., (1979). Improving Policing: A Problem-Oriented Approach. *Crime and Delinquency* 25: 236-258.

Goldstein, H., (1990). *Problem-Oriented Policing.* New York: McGraw-Hill.

Greenberg, D., and R. C. Kessler (1982). The Effects of Arrests on Crime: A Multivariate Panel Analysis. *Social Forces* 60: 771-90.

Greenberg, D. F., R. C. Kessler, and C. H. Logan (1979). A Panel Model of Crime Rates and Arrest Rates. *American Sociological Review* 44: 843-50.

Heal, K., and G. Laycock (1987). *Preventing Juvenile Crime: The Staffordshire Experience*. Police Research Group CPU Series Paper 8. London: Home Office.

Hirschel, D., I. W. Hutchison III, C. W. Dean, J. J. Kelley, and C. E. Pesackis (1990). *Charlotte Spouse Assault Replication Project: Final Report*. Charlotte, NC: University of North Carolina at Charlotte.

Holliday, L.P., (1974). *A Methodology For Radio Car Planning*. Unpublished Ms., New York City RAND Institute.

Hough M., (1996). *Drugs misuse and the Criminal Justice System: a review of the literature*. CDPU Paper 15. London: Home Office.

Huizinga, D., and F. Esbensen (1992). *School Safety* 15: 15-17.

Hurst, P., and P. Wright (1980). *Deterrence at Last: The Ministry of Transport's Alcohol Blitzes*. Paper Presented to the Eighth International Conference on Alcohol, Drugs and Traffic Safety, Stockholm.

Isaacs, H., (1967). *A Study of Communications, Crimes and Arrests in A Metropolitan Police Department*. Task Force Report: Science and Technology, A Report to the President's Commission on Law Enforcement and Administration of Justice. Washington, DC: USGPO.

Kansas City, MO, Missouri Police Department (1977). *Response Time Analysis*. Kansas City, MO.

Kelling, G. L., and C. M. Coles (1996). *Fixing Broken Windows: Restoring Order and Reducing Crime in Our Communities*. NY: Free Press.

Kelling, G. L., A. M. Pate, D. Dieckman and C. Brown (1974). *The Kansas City Preventive Patrol Experiment:* Technical Report. Washington, DC: Police Foundation.

Kleiman, M., (1988). Crackdowns: The Effects of Intensive Enforcement on Retail Heroin Dealing. In M. Chaiken, Ed., *Street-Level Drug Enforcement: Examining the Issues*. Washington, DC: National Institute of Justice.

Klein, M., (1986). Labelling Theory and Delinquency Policy: An Empirical Test. *Criminal Justice and Behavior* 13: 47-79.

Koper, C., (1995). *Just Enough Police Presence: Reducing Crime and Disorderly Behavior By Optimizing Patrol Time in Crime Hot Spots.*

Larson, R., (1975). What Happened to Patrol Operations in Kansas City. *Journal of Criminal Justice.* 3: 299-330.

Laycock, G., and N. Tilley (1995). *Policing and Neighbourhood Watch: Strategic Issues.* Police Research Group CDP Series Paper 60. London: Home Office.

Leigh A., T, Read and N. Tilley. *Problem-Oriented Policing: Brit Pop.* Police Research Group CDPS Paper 75. London: Home Office.

Lindsay, B., and D. McGillis (1986). Citywide Community Crime Prevention: An Assessment of the Seattle Program. In D. Rosenbaum, Ed., *Community Crime Prevention: Does It Work?* Beverly Hills, CA: Sage.

Logan, C. H., (1975). Arrest Rates and Deterrence. *Social Science Quarterly* 56: 376-89.

Marciniak, E., (1994). *Community Policing of Domestic Violence: Neighborhood Differences in the Effect of Arrest.* PhD Dissertation, University of Maryland.

Martin, S., and L. Sherman (1986). Selective Apprehension: A Police Strategy for Repeat Offenders. *Criminology* 24: 55-72.

Pate, A. M., and E. E. Hamilton (1992). Formal and Informal Deterrents to Domestic Violence: The Dade County Spouse Assault Experiment. American *Sociological Review.* 57: 691-698.

Pate, A. M., and W. Skogan (1985). *Coordinated Community Policing: The Newark Experience.* Technical Report. Washington, DC: Police Foundation.

Pate, A., A. Ferrara, R. A. Bowers, and J. Lorence (1976). *Police Response Time: Its Determinants and Effects.* Washington, DC: Police Foundation.

Pate, A. M., M. McPherson, and G. Silloway (1987). *The Minneapolis Community Crime Prevention Experiment:* Draft Evaluation Report. Washington, DC: Police Foundation.

Pate, A., E. E. Hamilton and S. Annan (1991). *Metro-Dade Spouse Abuse Replication Project*: Draft Final Report. Washington, D.C.: Police Foundation.

Paternoster, R., B. Brame, R. Bachman and L. W. Sherman (1996). Do Fair Procedures Matter? The Effect of Procedural Justice on Spouse Assault. *Law and Society Review*.

Pawson, R., and N. Tilley (1997) *Realistic Evaluation*. London: Sage

Police Foundation (1981). *The Newark Foot Patrol Experiment*. Washington, D.C.: Police Foundation.

Press, S.J., (1971). *Some Effects of an Increase in Police Manpower in the 20th Precinct of New York City*. NY: New York City Rand Institute.

Reiss, A. J. Jr., (1985). *Policing a City's Central District: The Oakland Story*. Washington, DC: National Institute of Justice.

Rosenbaum, D., D. A. Lewis and J. A. Grant (1986). Neighborhood-Based Crime Prevention: Assessing the Efficacy of Community Organizing in Chicago. In D. Rosenbaum, editor, *Community Crime Prevention: Does It Work?* Beverly Hills, CA: Sage.

Ross, H. L., (1973). Law, Science and Accidents: The British Road Safety Act of 1967. *Journal of Legal Studies* 2: 1-78.

Ross, H. L., (1975). The Scandinavian Myth: The Effectiveness of Drinking-and-Driving Legislation in Sweden and Norway. *Journal of Legal Studies* 4: 285-310.

Ross, H. L., (1977). Deterrence Regained: The Cheshire Constabulary's Breathalyser Blitz. *Journal of Legal Studies* 6: 241-249.

Ross, H. L., (1981). *Deterring the Drinking Driver: Legal Policy and Social Control.* Lexington, Mass: Lexington Books.

Ross, H. L., R. McCleary and T. Epperlein (1982). Deterrence of Drinking and Driving in France: An Evaluation of the Law of July 12, 1978. *Law and Society Review*.

Scarman, Lord (1981). *The Brixton Disorders 10–12 April 1981*. Report of an enquiry by the Rt Hon The Lord Scarman, OBE. Cmnd 8427. London: HMSO.

Schwartz, R., and J. Skolnick (1962). Two Studies of Legal Stigma. Social *Problems* 10: 133-138.

Sherman, L. W., (1990). Police Crackdowns: Initial and Residual Deterrence. In M. Tonry and N. Morris, Eds., *Crime and Justice: A Review of Research,* Vol. 12. Chicago: University of Chicago Press.

Sherman, L. W,. and R. A. Berk (1984). The Specific Deterrent Effects of Arrest for Domestic Assault. *American Sociological Review,* 49, 261-272.

Sherman, L. W., and D. P. Rogan (1995). Deterrent Effects of Police Raids on Crack Houses: A Randomized, Controlled, Experiment. *Justice Quarterly* 12: 755-781.

Sherman, L. W., et al., (1991). From Initial Deterrence to Long-Term Escalation: Short-Custody Arrest for Poverty Ghetto Domestic Violence. *Criminology* 29: 821-50.

Sherman, L., et al., (1992). The Variable Effects of Arrest on Criminal Careers: The Milwaukee Domestic Violence Experiment. *Journal of Criminal Law and Criminology* 83: 137-169.

Sherman, L., J. W. Shaw and D. P. Rogan (1995). *The Kansas City Gun Experiment*: Research in Brief. Washington, D.C.: National Institute of Justice.

Sherman, L. W. et al. (1997). *Preventing Crime: What works, what doesn't, what's promising.* Office of Justice Programs Research Report: U.S Department of Justice.

Skogan, W., (1990). *Disorder and Decline.* New York: Free Press.

Skogan, W., et al.(1995). *Community Policing In Chicago, Year Two.* Chicago: Illinois Criminal Justice Information Authority.

Smith D., and P. R. Gartin (1989). *Specifying Specific Deterrence: The Influence of Arrest on Future Criminal Activity.*

Spelman, W., and Brown, D. K. (1981). *Calling the Police: A Replication of the Citizen Reporting Component of the Kansas City Response Time Analysis. Washington,* DC: Police Executive Research Forum.

Sviridoff, M., et al. (1992). *The Neighborhood Effects of Street-Level Drug Enforcement: Tactical Narcotics Teams in New York.* NY: Vera Institute of Justice.

Tilley, N., (1993). After Kirkholt: *Theory, Methods and Results of Replication Evaluations.* Crime Prevention Unit Paper 47. London: Home Office.

Tittle, C. R., and A. R. Rowe (1974). Certainty of Arrest and Crime Rates: A Further Test of the Deterrence Hypothesis. *Social Forces* 52: 455-62.

Trojanowicz, R., (1986). Evaluating a Neighborhood Foot Patrol Program: The Flint, Michigan Project. In D. Rosenbaum, editor, *Community Crime Prevention: Does It Work?* Beverly Hills, CA: Sage.

Tyler, T., (1990). *Why People Obey the Law.* New Haven: Yale University Press.

Uchida, C. D., B. Forst and S. O. Annan (1992). *Modern Policing and the Control of Illegal Drugs: Testing New Strategies in Two American Cities.* Research Report. Washington, D.C.: National Institute of Justice.

Weisburd, D., and L. Green (1995). Policing Drug Hot Spots: The Jersey City Drug Market Analysis Experiment. *Justice Quarterly* 12: 711-735.

Wycoff, M. A., and W. Skogan (1986). Storefront Police Offices: The Houston Field Test. In D. Rosenbaum, editor, *Community Crime Prevention: Does It Work?* Beverly Hills, CA: Sage.

Wycoff, M. A., and W. Skogan (1993). *Community Policing in Madison: Quality from the Inside Out. An Evaluation of Implementation and Impact.* Research Report. Washington, D.C.: National Institute of Justice.

Wycoff, M. A., A. M. Pate, W. Skogan and L. W. Sherman (1985). *Citizen Contact Patrol in Houston: Executive Summary.* Washington, DC: Police Foundation.

Zimmer, L., (1990). Proactive Policing Against Street-Level Drug Trafficking. *American Journal of Police* 11: 43-74.

Section III

Criminal Justice interventions

7 The role of sentencing policy

David Moxon

Introduction

The aims of criminal justice interventions are wide ranging. They are principally to:

* apprehend and provide appropriate sanctions against offenders;

* ensure conviction of the guilty and acquittal of the innocent;

* change future behaviour of offenders for the better;

* deter those who might otherwise be tempted into crime; and,

* maintain public confidence in the criminal justice system.

This chapter reviews the options for dealing with offenders and the available evidence as to what they achieve. The options for dealing with an arrested suspect are to:

* give an informal warning, whereby a police officer warns an offender stopped or arrested for a minor offence of the consequences of further offending;

* administer a formal police caution;

* couple a formal caution with other measures – `caution plus';

* require participation in a restorative justice scheme, whereby some form of reparation is made. This may be linked to other measures, such as caution plus, or used on its own; and,

* prosecute – sentencing options are considered later.

Informal warnings

Informal warnings are the lowest level of police action, and are sometimes used where the need for any police intervention is borderline. They have assumed more prominence recently, as incidents which the police might previously have overlooked may now result in low-level action as part of a 'zero tolerance' strategy. They avoid 'legalistic' processing of juveniles, which can increase the risk of reoffending (see Chapter 6). However, as no record is kept it is not possible to measure the extent to which those given informal warnings get into trouble with the police again. In the zero tolerance context informal warnings are one strand in a wider strategy which is designed to demonstrate to would-be offenders that even low-level misbehaviour will not be tolerated, thereby preventing escalation into more serious crime. Evaluations of policing strategies will become available in the future, but separating out the influence of informal warnings will remain problematic. However, as informal warnings are very cheap there is no reason, on the available evidence, to discourage their use for trivial offences.

Cautioning

A caution is a formal warning administered by a police officer. Home Office guidance in 1994 made it clear that cautions would rarely be appropriate for repeat offenders, those accused of indictable-only offences or cases where there were aggravating factors. Cautions are most commonly used for young offenders, and in all age groups they are used proportionately more for females than males.

A study of reconviction rates for those cautioned in 1985, 1988 and 1991 showed that 15 per cent were convicted of a further offence within two years, and 28 per cent within five years (Home Office, 1994). The likelihood of conviction was strongly related to age and past history. Young people were much more likely to be convicted within two years than older people. Those with past cautions or convictions were much more likely to be convicted. Just under one-quarter of those with no previous cautions or convictions were convicted within five years, rising to three-quarters of those with three or more previous convictions.

For young offenders, there is no evidence that the reconviction rates are any higher than for a first conviction (Home Office, 1994); justice is dispensed more quickly; and the costs are far less than for more formal processing.

Caution plus

A caution plus comprises a formal caution with additional requirements. With some exceptions (see first example below) these schemes typically involve work with offenders to bring home to them the consequences of their actions, both for themselves and others, and to strengthen their ability to resist offending in the future. They can also involve an element of reparation to the victim. Examples of such requirements are:

- vehicle defect rectification schemes, whereby an offender with a minor vehicle defect is cautioned on condition that the defect is rectified;

- a scheme in Milton Keynes focuses on shop theft (McCulloch, 1996). Attending sessions is voluntary but there is a high level of take-up; and,

- a caution plus scheme in Northamptonshire arranges compensation for the victims and addresses offending behaviour. The cost is about one quarter that of the youth court process (Audit Commission, 1996).

These schemes have not yet been rigorously evaluated. In the Milton Keynes scheme only 13 per cent of those attending the Retail Theft Initiative (RTI) scheme are known to have reoffended (compared to 30 per cent of those cautioned and 64 per cent for those dealt with in other ways) However, these comparisons are affected by age, differences in follow-up and self-selection. In Northamptonshire, where payment of compensation was negotiated there was a much better record of payment than with court-ordered compensation. Reconviction rates were 35 per cent within 18 months. Although no formal comparison group is available, this is promising as few of those referred to the unit were first offenders. Victims were generally satisfied, and 40 per cent felt the approach was more appropriate than going to court compared with 20 per cent who would have preferred the court option.

Restorative justice

Restorative justice seeks to provide reparation to the victim, and to make the offender take responsibility for his or her actions. Its aims are to:

- restore the well-being of victims and of the community damaged by crime; and,

- prevent reoffending.

It is defined by Marshall (1997) as 'a process whereby all parties with a stake in a specific offence come together to resolve collectively how to deal with the aftermath of the offence and its implications for the future.' It often involves mediation sessions, involving both victim and offender, and some form of reparation to the victim. In some schemes the offender is diverted from formal proceedings, although it can be part of a court disposal or caution plus.

A study involving diversion of juveniles from court proceedings is being undertaken in Australia. Oxford University are using a similar model to evaluate a scheme which has been operating since 1995 in Thames Valley. Initial indications from both studies are that both victims and offenders consider them to be procedurally fair and victims tend to be more satisfied.

Sentencing

The main aims of sentencing are to:

- deter potential offenders from being drawn into crime;

- deter the offender from committing crimes in the future because of the unpleasant consequences;

- rehabilitate the offenders so that they no longer wish to commit crime, e.g. through programmes which get them off drugs or bring home to them the harm they do their victims;

- prevent people from committing crimes against the general public through incarceration or other restrictions on their movements;

- maintain public confidence in the criminal justice system by imposing punishment commensurate with the offence; and,

- deal fairly and equitably with those who come before the courts.

On occasions one of the objectives will override the others; for example an offender who is seen as a danger to the public, or whose crimes are heinous, will be imprisoned regardless of other considerations. More often, sentencers are seeking to balance different objectives. Although sentencers may have clear aims, they have very little information as to how the various options will contribute to those aims. As long ago as 1961 the Streatfeild Committee stated:

> "In our view the key to advance in this field is to recognise the fundamental difference between assessing culpability and pursuing

the other objectives of sentencing; namely that where the court is seeking to reform, to deter, or to protect, it is seeking to control future events rather than simply to pass judgement on past events. Unless the results of this observation are properly marshalled and systematically made available to the courts, sentences aimed at controlling future events are largely speculative and the courts can not even know if such objectives are practicable."

Rather more information is available now, though large gaps remain and sentencers are still often uncertain how particular objectives can best be pursued. This is particularly true where the case does not demand custody, and the likely impact of the choice of non-custodial penalty on future behaviour is a major concern.

Turning the offender away from crime

In terms of measuring how successful sentences are diverting offenders from offending again and setting them on a law-abiding path through reform are inseparable: except for a handful of self-report studies, both are measured by reconviction. The main caveats are set out below.

- *Equating reconviction with failure* – almost all studies take any subsequent reconviction as an indication of failure regardless of the nature of the individual's previous criminal career. For example, if a person has seven previous convictions within two years for burglary, then receives a probation order and subsequently is convicted once of a minor public order offence in the two year follow-up period, we might reasonably conclude that his/her behaviour has changed for the better.

- *Comparing rates for different sentences* – certain offender characteristics, for example, age or the number of previous convictions, influence both the likelihood of reoffending and the sentence. Thus first offenders are more likely to be fined, repeat offenders to receive probation. This means that those given different types of sentence have unequal chances of reconviction because of their history, and crude reconviction rates tell us little.

- *Reconviction is only a proxy measure of reoffending* – as the information is taken from police records, it only measures those offences which result in conviction. It has been estimated that for every 100 offences committed only two criminal convictions are obtained. As this ratio varies according to the type of offence committed, reconviction rates will be correspondingly affected.

Police practices, including whether they subject those with previous convictions to closer surveillance, will also affect conviction rates. There are higher reconviction rates for probationers given more intensive supervision. A current study by the National Institute of Justice is examining self-reported crime rates of offenders on probation to get round this problem (Mackenzie et al., 1997).

Despite their shortcomings, reconviction rates are the only accessible hard data normally available to measure reoffending and so they have been accepted as the basic criterion to measure the impact of different sentences on future behaviour.

Reconviction rates for different penalties

Comparison of custody and community penalties

When overall reconviction rates for custody are compared with those for community penalties, there is no significant difference in the effects of the disposals on reconviction rates (Kershaw and Renshaw, 1997). Other factors such as age, sex and previous criminal history have a bigger influence. Figure 7.1 shows that, when adjusted for key variables, the reconviction rates for custody and community penalties remained remarkably close over a number of years. The reconviction rate within two years of discharge from prison has fluctuated around 53 per cent since 1989 (when calculated on a comparable basis over time). This followed a fall from 58 per cent in 1987, coinciding with the diversion of young offenders from the courts.

When adjustments are made to reconviction rates for community penalties to achieve comparability with prison, these have been within two percentage points of the figures for prison throughout the period 1987-1995.

These adjustments take account of:

- differences in the characteristics of offenders commencing community penalties and those discharged from prison (e.g. age, sex, previous criminal history); and,

- the larger proportion of convictions following a community penalty that relate to offences committed before the order started, compared to the proportion of convictions following discharge from prison that relate to earlier offences (these were termed "pseudo-reconvictions" by Lloyd, Mair, and Hough, (1994)).

Figure 7.1 Reconviction rates within two years for those released from prison between 1987 and 1995 and adjusted¹ rates for those commencing community penalties² during this period

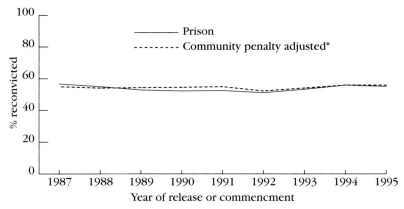

Notes:
1.   Adjusted to account for differences in the characteristics of offenders and for pseudo-reconvictions.
2   Figures for community penalties include combination orders from 1993 onwards and for 1995, are based only on commencements in the first quarter of the year.

Comparison of non-custodial sentences

Table 7.1 shows rates for various disposals, comparing actual rates for each disposal with those 'expected' on the basis of the age, sex and criminal history of offenders given that disposal.

Table 7.1 Two–year reconviction rates for those sentenced in 1993

Disposal	Actual rate %	'Expected' rate %
Conditional discharge	39	40
Fine	43	44
Probation	55	52
Community service	48	46

For those given conditional discharges or fined the actual reconviction rate is very slightly lower than the expected rate; for probation and community service orders it is slightly higher. However, because these figures relate to the date of conviction rather than the date of completion of the sentence, some of those reconvicted may only have committed further offences early in the life of the order before any benefits arising from contact with the probation service had time to take effect.

Community Service

Community Service (CS), introduced in England and Wales in 1975, can prevent further offending by re-integrating the offender into the community. National Standards for the Probation Service emphasise the punitive and reparative potential of Community Service – offenders are to undertake positive, demanding and socially useful unpaid work, keeping to disciplined requirements. Scope for encouraging a sense of personal responsibility and self-discipline is also recognised.

There has been no recent large-scale, reliable research on the effectiveness of community service in England and Wales, although Thomas et al. (1990) examined practices in five CS schemes. An evaluation of community service in Scotland (McIvor, 1992) has shown that:

• reconviction rates there compared favourably with those of similar offenders who were imprisoned;

• a high proportion of offenders felt that they acquired new skills and/or a sense of satisfaction with having helped someone through the tasks undertaken. Some felt that their self esteem and self confidence had increased (consistent with findings from Thomas et al. 1990);

• offenders who viewed the CS experience positively were less often reconvicted and fewer were convicted of property offences than those who found the experience less worthwhile; and,

• CS is popular with those involved, including social services (who are responsible for supervising offenders in the community in Scotland), judges and service recipients.

Although use of this disposal has increased steadily, the research indicates that there is little targeting on offenders likely to respond well, intake being governed by the need to gain 'numbers' (Hedderman and Sugg, 1997).

Electronic monitoring

Recently, curfew orders with electronic monitoring were introduced as a sentence in England and Wales, following their apparent success in the US, to meet the desire for new, credible community sentences. The evaluation of trials, begun in 1995, indicate (Mair and Mortimer, 1996; Mortimer and May 1997):

• the equipment was reliable;

- over three-quarters of orders were completed successfully; and,

- sentencers viewed them as a severe non-custodial penalty, imposed as a genuine alternative to custody and higher end community penalties. They were pleased at the speed with which breaches were detected.

The cost of a curfew order is likely to be higher than that of a community service order but less than a probation order. If imposed with a community sentence, however, the cost would exceed that for a probation order. Although it is difficult to compare the overall costs of curfew orders with custody, comparing average monthly costs indicates that the cost of a curfew order, including an element for probation supervision (£760) is between a third and a half that of custody. The monthly cost drops to £543 without supervision.

Sentence length

Reconviction rates following release from prison are generally lower as the length of the original sentence increases. Much of the reduction in rates among offenders with longer sentences is associated with their age, sex, age at first conviction and number of previous convictions. However, even after taking these factors into account, the rates for longer sentences are lower than would be expected. In part, this is thought to be due to other characteristics of offenders who are given longer sentences (such as the nature of the offences they commit). It also reflects the higher proportion of those on longer sentences who were released on parole/conditional discharge. There is evidence that these ex-prisoners have lower reconviction rates during post-release supervision and this reduces their overall reconviction rates. This suggests that once allowance is made for the characteristics of offenders receiving different sentences and the known beneficial effect of parole, there is no clear relationship between sentence length and propensity to reoffend.

General deterrence

Potential offenders may be deterred by their perceptions of:

- the risk of being caught and convicted; and,

- the severity of sentence on conviction.

Potential offenders may well have very little idea as to the risk of being caught, or about the likely severity of any punishment if they are convicted.

Any increases in the likelihood of being caught or the severity of punishment can only have a deterrent effect if perceptions change as well. Deterrence will also depend on how potential offenders view the consequences of a more severe penalty (for example, if they discount remote future consequences more heavily than immediate rewards or satisfaction). It is therefore difficult to measure deterrence directly and most currently available evidence is from studies of statistical associations. In these it is not generally obvious how much of any effect is due to deterrence and how much to incapacitation. Various types of association study have been attempted.

Some researchers have looked at geographic comparisons between areas with different sentencing policies (e.g. Farrington and Langan, 1997). However in these studies is difficult to obtain comparability between measures and to disentangle sentencing from other simultaneous events differentiating the areas studied. Others have looked at dramatic changes in legislation, such as "Three strikes and you're out". In a recent study of California Stolzenberg and D'Alessio (1997) could find no impact on crime rates.

A further technique is to use econometric methods. Levitt (1996) studied the effect on crime rates of changes in punishment severity (using prison overcrowding litigation as a means of controlling for simultaneous effects). He found that reduced severity was associated with increased crime, particularly burglary and larceny. However, he does not convincingly demonstrate the causal sequence, in particular that pre-existing crime rates or punishment rates had no influence on overcrowding. An earlier study by Reilly and Witt (1996) compared length of imprisonment with 12 years' data for 42 English police forces (crime, clear-ups and unemployment levels). They found an association between severity and crime, particularly burglary and robbery. However the analysis also contained some negative associations and took no account of differences in the likelihood of imprisonment between areas.

Thus, although there is some evidence of an association between severity and crime rates, much of it is ambiguous and none yet enables us to quantify deterrence effects separately from incapacitation. A more detailed analysis will appear in a literature review commissioned by the Home Office Research and Statistics Directorate.

Incapacitation

In assessing the extent to which imprisonment contributes directly to crime reduction, one needs to know how many crimes an individual would be committing if they were at liberty. The incapacitation effects of custody are not easy to measure. They are affected by factors such as:

- the extent to which the workings of the criminal justice system succeed in placing the more prolific offenders in prison: a proportion of those caught would not have reoffended but some commit on average a crime a day;

- the value of crimes avoided – numbers of crimes are a very partial measure which takes no account of the injury, loss or damage they cause; and,

- the way crimes are measured – different measures will yield different results, and in particular recorded crime will produce a lower figure for crimes avoided than estimates based on victim surveys.

Tarling (1994) estimated that a 25 per cent increase in the prison population would be necessary to obtain a one per cent fall in the crime rate (based on levels of imprisonment and crime prevailing at that time). This translates into just under five recorded crimes per addition to the prison population, or around 13 crimes measured by the British Crime Survey. This in turn excludes crimes against businesses, which might push the figure up to around 20 crimes prevented for each addition to the prison population. Estimates from the US have suggested a stronger incapacitation effect, with crime rates falling by between 0.12 per cent and 0.2 per cent, with a best estimate of 0.16 per cent, for every one per cent increase in the custodial population. An important reason for the difference is that the US prison population is much larger than ours: adding 25 per cent to the US prison population would mean an extra 400,000 inmates which will have a much larger effect on crime than adding 25 per cent – some 16,000 people – to our prison population.

Maintaining public confidence

Recent years have seen an increase in the use of imprisonment, both in terms of the numbers of people imprisoned and average sentence lengths. This increasing severity has been driven by various factors, including political pressure and, linked to this, perceived public demand for tougher punishment. A recent study of attitudes to sentencing (Hough and Roberts, 1998) showed that the public felt that sentencers were out of touch and imposed excessively lenient sentences. However, when presented with an example of a real case, along with the sentencing options, the sentences respondents imposed were similar to, or more lenient than, the sentence imposed in the real life case. To a large extent, therefore, the pressure on sentencers to treat offenders more severely is driven by misconceptions as to what they actually do. The point is reinforced by the fact that a study for the Royal Commission on Criminal Justice, which involved interviews with all participants in Crown Court cases, found that those who had sat through the cases were in broad agreement with the sentencing decisions in the cases they observed (Zander and Henderson, 1993).

If sentencing practices are to have a deterrent effect on potential offenders and if the influence of public opinion on potential changes in sentencing policy is to be evidence based, there is an important job to be done in terms of educating the public as to what the sentencing process actually delivers, and at what cost.

Equity of treatment

In the main, sentencers have very wide discretion. With a very few exceptions, there are no minimum sentences. Maximum sentences tend to be much more severe than would be considered in more than a tiny fraction of cases. In magistrates' courts, sentencers can draw on the Magistrates' Association guidelines which suggest starting points for different offences, and list aggravating and mitigating factors. At the Crown Court, the Court of Appeal has a role in establishing appropriate sentences through the way it deals with cases referred to it. Nevertheless, there are wide variations in the use of different types of sentence for given classes of offence between different courts (Justices Clerks' Society et al., 1997). This variation between courts suggests a need for tighter guidelines which could be developed with more regard to the costs and impact of different types of sentence. The central point here is that the discussion of overall sentencing levels is an average constructed from a very wide range of sentencing practices.

Costs of disposals

The costs of different disposals are set out in Table 7.2. The figures are average costs, which are appropriate for costing the effects of sentencing policy and practice. These take account of the fact that people sentenced to custody tend to serve no more than about half of the length of sentence imposed. The figures are costs to criminal justice agencies, mainly to the prison and probation services. There may be other costs (e.g. loss of economic output of someone in prison) or benefits (e.g. work done under community service orders).

Table 7.2 Effectiveness of sentences and other interventions

	Aim				Cost	Impact
	General deterrence	Individual deterrence	Incapac- itation	Reform		
Interventions						
Informal warning		X			£2.50	Not known
Caution		X			£18.30	Low reoffending for first offenders
Caution plus		X		X	Note 1	Promising in terms of reoffending
Restorative justice		X		X	Note 1	Promising in terms of reoffending

	Aim				Cost	Reoffending
	General deterrence	Individual deterrence	Incapac- itation	Reform		(see note 2)
Sentence						
Discharge		X			£0	1
Fine	X	X			-£137	1
Probation	X	X		X	£2,527	-3
Community service	X	X		X	£1,628	-2
Combination order	X	X		X	£3,588	-4
Imprisonment	X	X	X	X	Note 3	

Notes:
1. Costs of caution plus restorative justice schemes are extremely variable, not least because they are targeted at different groups and require very different levels of professional input. The cost of the Northamptonshire scheme was £625 for each person referred.
2. Figures for reoffending indicate improvement over expected reconviction rate (measured in terms of the difference between the two percentages).
3. Cost per sentence is not available for prisons. However the gross cost of a prison place is £37,500 per year (this includes capital costs).

Cost of prosecution

Magistrates' court timeous guilty plea	£600
Magistrates' court not guilty plea	£1,600
Crown Court timeous guilty plea	£2,100
Late guilty plea	£6,300
Crown Court not guilty plea	£16,650

Note: Full committal hearings add £1,950 to the average cost of a Crown Court case. A paper committal adds £1,150.

Conclusions

Such evidence as we have, from a range of schemes in different countries, suggests projects involving some form of reparation and which confront offenders with the consequences of their behaviour are promising. Interventions of this sort may be particularly productive with young offenders, who are at most risk of reoffending and may be least inclined to think about consequences.

Reconviction studies over the years have told a consistent story. There is little difference between sentences in terms of their impact on reoffending rates. Other factors, such as the age and criminal history of the offender, are much more strongly associated with differences in reconviction rates. These findings are at a general level, and it would be wrong to conclude that individual programmes within prisons or run by the Probation Service may not have an effect, as the next section shows.

Custody is the most expensive disposal and, once the prisoner is released, is no more successful at preventing further crimes than other disposals. But it protects the public from the risk of further harm while the imprisonment lasts, and satisfies the public need for retribution in respect of serious offenders. With only limited estimates of offences prevented by imprisonment and rather less known about the cost of those offences to the community, the cost-effectiveness of imprisonment in terms of crime control cannot be assessed with any degree of reliability.

It makes sense for the choice between non-custodial disposals to be based in large measure on the likely consequences on future behaviour. It is difficult to see much justification for opting for an expensive community penalty if the outcome in terms of future offending is no better than a fine. As the next chapter shows, there are probation programmes which can have an impact on offending but these tend to require more resources than straight probation (which does not appear to have much effect on offending). A central conclusion, therefore, is that the resources of the Probation Service should not be dissipated on those for whom a fine would serve as well. To do so may have the perverse effect of diluting the impact that the Probation Service can have on those for whom some form of intensive intervention would bear fruit. Reconviction rates for fines compare favourably with community penalties. There is thus no evidence that the switch from fines to community penalties that has occurred over the past 20 years has achieved anything by way of crime reduction.

References

Audit Commission (1996) *Misspent Youth...young people and crime.* London: Audit Commission for Local Authorities and the National Health Service in England and Wales.

Farrington D. P., and P. A. Langan (1997). *Crime and Punishment in America and England.* Final Report to the Bureau of Justice Statistics, Washington D.C.

Hedderman, C., and Sugg, D., (1997) *Changing offenders' attitudes and behaviour: what works?* Home Office Research Study 171. London: Home Office.

Home Office (1994). *The Criminal Histories of Those Cautioned in 1985, 1988 and 1991.* Home Office Statistical Bulletin 8/94. London: Home Office.

Hough, M., and Roberts, J., (1998) *Attitudes to punishment: findings from the British Crime Survey.* Home Office Research Study 179. London: Home Office.

Justices' Clerks' Society, Magistrates Association and Home Office (1997). *Local Sentencing Patterns in Magistrates' Courts 1996.* Home Office Research and Statistics Directorate. London: Home Office.

Levitt, S., (1996) Effect of Prison Population Rates on Crime Rates: Evidence from Prison Overcrowding Litigation. *Quarterly Journal of Economics,* 111, 319-352.

Lloyd, C., Mair, G, and Hough, M., (1994) *Explaining reconviction rates: a critical analysis.* Home Office Research Study 136. London: HMSO.

Kershaw, C., and Renshaw, G., (1997). *Reconvictions of prisoners discharged from prison in 1993,* England and Wales. Home Office Statistical Bulletin 5/97. London: Home Office.

Mair, G., and Mortimer, E., (1996). *Curfew orders with electronic monitoring: an evaluation of the first twelve months of the trials in Greater Manchester, Norfolk and Berkshire, 1995-1996.* Home Office Research Study 163. London: Home Office.

Marshall, A., (1997). *Integrating Restorative Justice into the Criminal Justice System: Implications for the Comprehensive Spending Review.*

McCulloch H., (1996). *Shop Theft: Improving the Police Response.* Police Research Group CDPS Paper No. 76. London: Home Office.

McIvor, G., (1992) *"Sentenced to Serve: The operation and impact of community service by Offenders"*: Avebury, Aldershot.

Mackenzie, L., Browning, K., Priu H., Skroban S., Smith, D., (1997). *Probation as Public Safety Protection: Evidence from Self Reports.* University of Maryland.

Mortimer, E., and May, C., (1997). *Electronic Monitoring in Practice: the Second Year of the Trials of Curfew Orders.* Home Office Research Study 177. London: HMSO.

Reilly, B., and R. Witt (1996). Crime Deterrence and Unemployment in England and Wales: an an empirical analysis. *Bulletin of Economic Research,* 48, 137-159.

Stolzenberg, L., and S. D'Alessio (1997). "Three Strikes and You're Out". The Impact of California's new Mandatory Sentencing Law on Serious Crime Rates. *Crime and Delinquency,* 43, 457-469.

Streatfeild Committee (1961). *The Business of the Criminal Courts.* London: HMSO.

Tarling R., (1994). *Analysing Offending. Data, Models and Interpretations.* London: HMSO.

Thomas, N., Hine, J., and Nugent, M., (1990) *Study of Community Service Orders: Summary Report.* Unpublished report to the Home Office.

Zander M., and Henderson P., (1993) *Royal Commission on Criminal Justice Research Study No. 19: Crown Court Study.* London: HMSO.

8 Effective interventions with offenders

Julie Vennard and Carol Hedderman

Introduction

This chapter summarises the main messages from research regarding the effectiveness in reducing further offending of different types of intervention undertaken in prison or in the community. There is currently a commitment to increasing the number of offenders attending programmes designed and delivered to principles of effective practice in both settings. We examine here what types of intervention (and methods of delivery) achieve reductions in reoffending and how the impact of the more promising programmes can be increased.

In sending an offender to prison the sentencer's main objectives are to punish, incapacitate, mark society's disapproval and, perhaps, deter. In the case of community sentences the intention may be to combine punishment – in the form of restriction of liberty – with reparation and rehabilitation. A recent (unpublished) Home Office survey of magistrates' views of the purpose of community sentences and what they can achieve was carried in two English probation areas. This indicated that the majority believed that community sentences can rehabilitate. Eight out of ten thought that both probation and combination orders could reduce reoffending through efforts to address offending behaviour, with combination orders also providing reparation and restriction of liberty. In contrast only a quarter thought that prison could rehabilitate, but all respondents thought it restricted liberty and eight out of ten thought it could deter effectively.

There have been major shifts since 1980 in official and professional thinking about the purpose of community penalties, reflected in the types of question addressed in probation research (Raynor, 1997). Increasing optimism about the rehabilitative potential of community sentences can be attributed largely to the findings from Canadian and North American research. As Raynor (1997) points out, however, the 'toughening up' of community sanctions as a result of the Criminal Justice Act 1991 and the subsequent National Standards have also contributed to the search for more effective forms of supervision.

Given the increasing emphasis on the ability of community sentences to rehabilitate, it is not surprising that reconviction rates have come to be relied upon as a key measure of their success or failure in reducing offending behaviour. However, the case for drawing on other measures has been widely argued, not least because reconviction rates have a number of limitations (Lloyd et al., 1994). These were described in Chapter 7 and may be summarised as:

- reconviction rates do not take into account changes in offence severity or a reduction in the frequency of offending;

- reconviction rates under-estimate the true level of *reoffending* since for many types of offence the clear-up rate is very low;

- police forces have differing clear-up rates which reflect differences in the chances of being arrested and reconvicted;

- there is lack of consistency in the length of follow-up period used in reconviction studies; although two years is widely used, for sex offenders five years is considered desirable and for burglars six months to a year may be adequate; and,

- in the case of custodial sentences the follow-up period begins at the date of release, whereas for community penalties counting begins on the date of sentence.

In this chapter, reconviction rates are reported, where known, but other outcome measures are also considered such as attitudinal and behavioural change or success in dealing with specific problems associated with offending behaviour.

The effectiveness of different types of intervention

The broad comparisons between the reconviction rates for different sentences reported in Chapter 7 have been widely interpreted as indicating that type of sentence, of itself, has little or no impact on the likelihood of reoffending. It is important to remember, however, that these comparisons do not provide a guide to the effectiveness of any specific interventions delivered during these sentences.

Increasing pressure on both the Prison and Probation Services to demonstrate that the offending behaviour programmes they run are successful can be attributed to a number of developments over the last decade, notably:

- a 39 per cent increase in the number of offenders beginning community sentences - to around 118,200 offenders in 1997;

- an increase in the proportion of these offenders and those supervised on release from custody who were convicted of serious offences;

- new community sentences (combination orders and curfew orders with electronic monitoring) have been introduced;

- a new concern with the comparative effectiveness of all forms of sentence, (Lloyd et. al. 1994) and in the increasing desire to draw practical lessons from research (e.g., 'Managing What Works' Conference, 1995); and,

- increasing use of performance targets in the Prison Service e.g. the provision of positive regimes to address offending behaviour (Prison Service Corporate Plan 1995-98).

In this context, many probation managers and practitioners have come to acknowledge the need to demonstrate that community sentences are effective in reducing reoffending. To this end, services have begun to set up systems to monitor the way they are delivering programmes; and some are attempting to evaluate their effectiveness. This approach is officially endorsed in guidance to Chief Probation Officers and Prison Service Governors.

The principles of effective work with offenders which are being promoted by both services are underpinned by research. Most of the studies in this field are North American and Canadian and care is needed when extrapolating from results found in one jurisdiction to another. The following 'what works' principles are, however, sufficiently broad for this not to be an issue:

- *risk classification* – more intensive programmes should be targeted at high risk offenders, while those of lower risk should receive lower or minimal intervention;

- *targeting 'criminogenic' needs* – researchers such as Andrews and Bonta (1994), Motiuk (1997) and Hollin and Palmer (1995) emphasise the importance of differentiating between those (criminogenic) factors which contribute directly to criminal behaviour (such as anti-social attitudes, drug dependency, low level educational and vocational skills, poor cognitive and interpersonal skills) and those which have a less direct relationship with propensity to reoffend (e.g. unsatisfactory accommodation). If the purpose of a programme is to reduce offending the focus has to be upon criminogenic needs;

- *programme integrity* – programmes should be properly carried out by trained staff in accordance with aims and objectives that do not change;

- *responsivity* – traditionally probation work has involved individual counselling, but research shows that the best results are obtained if teaching styles match offenders' learning styles – and most offenders require active, participatory approaches (e.g. role play), rather than loose, unstructured or overly didactic methods (e.g. Andrews, 1995);

- *treatment modality* – the most effective type of interventions are ones which are skills-based, designed to improve problem-solving and social interaction and which also include a cognitive component to address attitudes, values and beliefs which support offending behaviour (e.g. Lipsey, 1992); and,

- *community base* – generally community-based programmes have shown more positive results, but programmes which take into account the other five principles can be successful in reducing offending in any treatment setting (see, e.g., Andrews, 1995).

Guidance issued in 1995 to Chief Probation Officers and to Prison Governors also drew attention to organisational factors which are considered to be critical to effective practice. These included: senior management accountability for the activity or programme; adequate resourcing; staff who are appropriately trained and supported; and monitoring and evaluation of programme delivery. In addition, the Prison Service has begun to implement a system of accreditation for offending behaviour programmes, including those designed for sex offenders. Prison Governors have been advised that the research evidence strongly supports a presumption in favour of sustaining both the coverage and quality of sex offender and cognitive skills programmes.

Cognitive behavioural work with offenders

As an approach to addressing offending behaviour, 'cognitive-behavioural' modification is based on social learning theory. It assumes offenders are shaped by their environment and have failed to acquire certain cognitive skills or have learnt inappropriate ways of behaving. Their thinking may be impulsive and egocentric and their attitudes, values and beliefs may support anti-social behaviour. By drawing on a range of well-established cognitive and behavioural techniques offenders are helped to face up to the consequences of their actions, to understand their motives, and to develop new ways of controlling their behaviour (McGuire, 1996).

Cognitive-behavioural approaches are frequently used as part of a wider programme of work which includes problem-solving training, social skills training, and pro-social modelling with positive reinforcement of non-criminal behaviour or attitudes. Such programmes are increasingly seen as offering the best chance of success in reducing reoffending since they address such a broad range of needs and problems.

As many probation services are now adopting cognitive-behavioural approaches in their work with offenders, the Home Office Research and Statistics Directorate (RSD) recently reviewed the literature on the use and effectiveness of such techniques and examined how far services are running programmes which conform to the principles summarised above. (Vennard, Sugg and Hedderman, 1997; and Hedderman and Sugg, 1997). The literature review focused upon studies which have already been synthesised in reviews, some of which have used the technique of meta-analysis to aggregate the results of a large number of studies which, alone, may be too small to be of much value (e.g., Lipsey, 1992, Andrews et al., 1990).

Vennard et al. reported broad agreement that the most effective programmes for addressing offending behaviour by adults and juveniles are skills-based, designed to improve problem-solving, and draw on behavioural techniques to reinforce improved conduct. The lessons which can be drawn from the literature are therefore fairly general. They do not seek to identify which components or combinations work best, in what settings and under what conditions, with different types of offender. Nevertheless, there are consistent indications that:

- cognitive behavioural approaches, including role play, positive reinforcement and modification of dysfunctional attitudes, values and beliefs, are more successful than techniques such as unfocused group or individual counselling and unstructured therapy;

- cognitive-behavioural programmes, when delivered non-selectively to a broad range of offenders, achieve a 10-15 percentage point lower reconviction rate than that reported for similar offenders who did not attend such programmes;

- larger percentage point reductions in recidivism (typically around 20 percentage points lower than control groups) have been reported for programmes which follow the effectiveness principles closely (including targeting high risk offenders); and,

- programmes which also include training in social skills (for example, teaching sex offenders to form appropriate relationships with other adults) show the most positive results with both juvenile and adult offenders.

Although Probation Services in England and Wales frequently incorporate cognitive-behavioural or cognitive skills approaches in their work with offenders (39 areas who responded to the RSD survey ran 191 such programmes in 1996) the survey showed (Hedderman and Sugg, 1997):

- programme integrity was poor and staff training was inadequate;

- despite evidence that specialised programmes were more effective, general programmes were more popular. There was little sign that offenders were selected on the basis of need or risk as 'what works' principles recommend; and,

- specialist programmes are expensive but areas have spent little on examining whether they work.

The Prison Service has introduced two cognitive skills programmes in a number of prisons. One of these, the *Reasoning and Rehabilitation Programme (R and R)*, is also being drawn upon by several probation services. Developed in Canada, the R and R programme is widely used in other jurisdictions with high risk offenders (see Ross et al., 1998). A study by Robinson (1995) of the impact of the programme on a sample of Canadian offenders indicated that the R and R programme worked for both high and low risk offenders in community settings but only with high-risk violent and sexual offenders in prison. Non-violent property offenders and robbery offenders showed little response to the programme.

The R and R programme is running in approximately 20 establishments and a second cognitive programme, entitled *Enhanced Thinking Skills (ETS)* is in use in some 50 establishments. The Prison Service is evaluating the success of the two cognitive behavioural programmes in improving cognitive skills and, in the longer term, in reducing reconvictions. Initial results for the *ETS* programme indicate improved cognitive skill levels that are maintained for at least a year after completion of the programme.

Work with sex offenders

The RSD survey of probation areas (Hedderman and Sugg, 1997) also showed that sex offender programmes tend to be (comparatively) well-organised, run by well-trained staff, and draw on outside expertise. In part, this may reflect the fact that sex offender treatment programmes were among the first to make use of cognitive-behavioural approaches in this country, both in the community and in prison. However, it is also likely that areas have responded to the results of another RSD study (the 'STEP' project) which examined the impact of seven community-based treatment programmes for sex offenders (Beckett et al., 1994; Hedderman and Sugg, 1996).

The results of the STEP project showed that the long-term residential programme made most progress in changing attitudes. This was partly because the amount of time offenders spent being treated (average = 462 hours) was seven or eight times greater than in any other programme and partly because the programme focused on highly deviant child molesters rather than the broader range in other programmes.

This study also showed that those who went through treatment were less likely than a comparable untreated sample to have been reconvicted and attitudinal change was associated with this improvement. However, the numbers are fairly small and we know that for many sex offenders the period between reconvictions is lengthy.

The Prison Service has also developed a comparable sex offender treatment programme (SOTP) as part of a national strategy for the integrated assessment and treatment of sexual offenders (Thornton, 1991; Grubin and Thornton, 1994). It is too early to say whether the programme is successful in reducing reoffending but a nine month follow-up has shown that positive cognitive and attitudinal changes have held up well.

Treating drug offenders

Although the precise causal relationship between drug use and acquisitive crime is complex, a growing number of studies report that problem drug users rely heavily on the income they derive from crime to finance their drug habits (Hough, 1996). Other costs fall to the criminal justice, social security and health systems. There is some evidence, principally from North American studies, that treatment programmes (such as methadone maintenance) located within the criminal justice system can reduce illegal drug use and drug related crime (Hough, 1996; McMurran, 1996) although questions remain concerning which approaches work best for different types of offenders. Hough's review of the research literature on the links between drug misuse and crime and effective interventions within the criminal justice system has identified a number of findings specifically relating to community-based treatment (Hough, 1996). The research suggests that:

- legally coerced treatment accepted as a condition of an order can be as effective as treatment entered into 'voluntarily';

- drug testing can help in identifying illegal drug use and securing compliance with treatment conditions; and,

- drug testing should form an integral part of treatment, rather than being used simply as a form of surveillance.

To be successful such treatment must also ensure that problem users enter treatment quickly; stay in treatment for as long as possible (a minimum of three months) and are treated in a positive and supportive environment. Hough's literature review also highlights the importance of effective referral structures to build bridges between the criminal justice system and treatment services. Early (unpublished) results of an ongoing study by South Bank University of arrest referral schemes for problem drug users confirm that such schemes need to be pro-active and properly resourced, with drug workers having direct access to offenders (Edmunds et.al., 1997). Simply providing information about drug agencies results in low take-up. Tentative conclusions concerning the cost-effectiveness of referral schemes are that successful referral, resulting in contact with treatment agencies, can pay for itself through reductions in social security benefits and in crimes recorded by the police; savings may also accrue to the health service.

The Prison Service has made a recent significant investment in developing and piloting a range of drug treatment and rehabilitation services. As yet there are no results from these pilot studies. But a preliminary evaluation of a drug treatment programme introduced at HMP Downview in 1992 produced promising results in terms of abstinence from drug and alcohol use in the short term (Player and Martin, 1996). Positive change in attitudes to families and offending behaviour were also reported by those who remained in treatment.

Education and training

While much research effort has been devoted to examining which forms of treatment are effective in changing attitudes and behaviour, there has also been interest in examining what impact on reoffending can be achieved by providing help with practical problems – in particular those stemming from poor educational attainment and unemployment. Offenders serving custodial and community sentences are considerably more likely than the general population to be *poorly educated* (commonly with low levels of literacy), have few qualifications and skills, and to be *unemployed*. Although establishing a causative link between unemployment and offending is problematic, there is evidence that ex-prisoners and probationers are more likely to re-offend if they are unemployed (Crow et al., 1989; Simon and Corbett, 1996). Work done by RSD to develop reconviction prediction scores finds, consistently, that offenders who have had a reasonably stable record of employment are rather less likely to reoffend than those who have not (see also Farrington (1995) report of the key findings from the Cambridge Study in Delinquent Development).

As most jobs now require literacy levels above those achieved by many offenders, improvements in literacy and numeracy are an essential aid to post-release employment. A recent study in Canada has shown a substantial reduction in reoffending among those attending basic literacy and numeracy courses (Porporino and Robinson, 1992), with a major benefit seen as the help it provided in gaining and sustaining full-time employment. This suggests that the reduction in reoffending may depend crucially on employment opportunities.

It is difficult to demonstrate that *work experience and training* whilst in custody or on probation reduces re-offending. Hollin and Palmer (1995) were unable to find clear evidence that prison education and work programmes were associated with a lower rate of re-offending and Simon and Corbett (1996) were unable to establish any beneficial effect resulting from work and training in prison. There is, however, some evidence from evaluations of the impact of 'boot camp' regimes on recidivism (e.g. MacKenzie et al, 1995). Those which are effective include a greater element of education/training and throughcare links with the community. One of the main messages from the research is that prisons should work more closely with outside employers and should plan their provision to match labour market needs.

Probation Services are required to implement a policy on *employment, training and education* and are encouraged to strengthen their links with the Employment Services and with Training and Enterprise Councils (TECS) to help offenders back into training and work. Home Office funded research has examined the ways in which the TEC initiatives operate and identified a number of factors crucial to effective practice (Roberts et al., 1996). The timescale for the research did not permit an examination of their effectiveness in helping offenders find stable employment but a two year reconviction follow-up is underway.

Supervision by the Probation Service following release from prison

The Criminal Justice Act 1991 introduced compulsory post-release supervision by the Probation Service for all offenders sentenced to terms of imprisonment of 12 months and over. Those serving sentences of under four years are automatically released at the half-way point in their sentence (ACR). Discretionary release (DCR) on the recommendation of the Parole Board being reserved for prisoners serving four years and over. Offenders sentenced to less than twelve months do not receive statutory supervision but are eligible for voluntary after-care (VAC).

In a study of the first two years of ACR, Maguire, Peroud and Raynor (1996) observe that the principle of 'throughcare' now plays a central part in the ACR system, but they were unable to obtain an accurate picture of its effect on reconviction rates. Although rates were well below those expected, they were based on small numbers (91 cases) and probably reflected some under-recording. The authors noted that similar differences between expected and actual reconviction rates have been reported for parolees under supervision.

By its very nature, DCR selects for early release prisoners who tend to have a lower than average risk of reconviction. A few studies in this country and in America have sought to disentangle the 'selection' effect from the beneficial effect of different licence periods (Nuttall, 1977; Flannagan, 1982; Ward, 1987; Hann, 1991; Ditchfield, 1989). More recently Marshall (1995) compared the expected and actual reconviction rates for a large sample of parolees released on licence. Although inconclusive, the literature as a whole indicates that:

- having adjusted for risk factors, those released on parole still have lower rates of reconviction than those not paroled;

- the difference between expected and actual rates is slightly greater for more serious reoffending; and,

- the reasons for the apparent 'parole effect' remain unclear. Supervision/treatment and deterrence for the duration of the parole licence may all play a part in explaining the reduction in reconviction rates that persists after taking account of selection effects.

Improving the effectiveness of work with offenders

The research studies above have identified many ways in which the effectiveness of rehabilitative interventions with offenders might be enhanced. Some of these are already being addressed:

Assessing risk and need

More attention needs to be paid to systems for *assessing criminogenic needs* and *risk of reoffending*. Statistical risk predictors are increasingly available for use in this process (Copas and Marshall, 1998) and scales have been developed for assessing risk and need which detect changes in targeted attitudes and behaviour over time, such as the Level of Service Inventory (LSI-R).

Maintenance and relapse prevention

The importance of post-release risk management and reinforcement of what has been learned during the course of a programme is well established in the case of addictive behaviours, such as child sexual abuse and drug misuse. Maintenance groups or individual support are widely accepted methods of seeking to minimise the risk of relapse in the case of addictive behaviours. It may be that other types of offenders who have completed group work programmes in custody and in the community require improved follow-up support and reinforcement of what has been learned to ensure that beneficial changes are sustained. Raynor and Vanstone (1996) found that favourable one-year reconviction rates for a sample of offenders completing the Reasoning and Rehabilitation programme were no longer evident at the end of the second year following completion. They consider that better results might have been achieved if probation officers had continued to work beyond the programme on the thinking and related behaviour of the offenders known to be at high risk of further offending.

Accreditation

A system of accreditation of programmes can help to achieve a common core of high quality programmes and support effective methods of delivery. Now an accepted policy within the Prison Service and currently being developed for Probation Services, accreditation of programmes should overcome many of the problems identified in the research literature including:

- failure to make explicit how the intervention is supposed to work;

- lack of programme integrity; and,

- failure to monitor and evaluate.

Social factors and offending

The current emphasis on psychological explanations of criminal behaviour does not deny the central importance of environmental factors and childhood experiences, such as harsh and inconsistent parenting, time spent in care and poor educational attainment. An impoverished childhood may, for example, explain why an individual fails to acquire certain cognitive skills, acts impulsively or is unable to empathise with others. Because early experiences are so crucial, interventions later in life may have limited impact. Even fairly lengthy and well targeted interventions are, as Lösel (1995) puts it, 'only one episode in a long development of criminogenic habits and lifestyles'. This fact may partly explain the modest statistical effects reported in many of the more robust studies reported in the 'what works' research literature.

Research also suggests that, in this country, probation officers are more receptive towards an approach which explicitly recognises the role of current social problems in explaining further offending and expects the service to tackle these problems as well as cognitive deficits (Burnett, 1996; Mair and May, 1997). There is, moreover, increasing evidence that interventions with high risk young offenders are more effective if they address the links between personal (including cognitive) and social (family, peer group and school) problems (e.g. Borduin et al., 1995).

Monitoring and evaluation

The research literature suggests that programmes which draw on cognitive skills and behavioural methods are the more promising, consistently achieving reductions in reconviction which exceed those for control groups. However, it remains unclear precisely what sorts of technique work best, under what conditions with different types of offender. Programmes should be:

- monitored to check whether they target the right people and maintain treatment integrity

- delivered consistently by different members of staff; and,

- rigorously evaluated to assess impact (on attitudes, behaviour, skills, social problems and reconvictions), process (including duration and intensity of the work needed to effect change with different groups of offenders and why some offenders benefit more than others from the intervention) and costs.

The cost-effectiveness of offender rehabilitation programmes

Estimated expenditure on the Prison Service for 1997-98 (£1,257m) is more than four times that estimated for the Probation Service (£429m), even though the current caseload for the Probation Service is twice as high as the number of offenders serving prison sentences. Prison places cost considerably more than probation supervision and there are obvious economic reasons for attempting to reverse the growth of the prison population through wider use of community penalties. A cost-effectiveness analysis must, however, take into account important differences between the two services in the objectives they seek to achieve. While sharing some common purposes – main aims of both services are to reduce offending and protect the public – there are fundamental differences of emphasis and approach:

- custodial sentences ensure a higher level of public protection for the duration of the sentence;

- most offenders and members of the public would view community penalties as a less severe punishment than custody; and,

- sentencers have more confidence in the rehabilitative potential of community sentences.

It is beyond the scope of this chapter to attempt a full cost-effectiveness comparison between the two types of sentence. The limited information available on costs and outcomes means that it not even possible to compare the cost-effectiveness of offending behaviour programmes delivered in custody and in the community.

The lack of well developed systems for monitoring community-based programmes for offenders means that very few probation areas can supply reliable information on the costs of individual programmes they run. For example, the inspection of probation orders with additional requirements referred to earlier reported wide variation in per capita cost of places occupied at a probation centre, but cautioned against drawing inferences regarding value for money. The inspection discovered large differences in what services included in their cost calculations. The RSD survey of cognitive behavioural programmes (Hedderman and Sugg, 1997) confirmed this problem. Even the few areas which held cost information varied according to how they calculated the costs, so that they ranged from £61,000 to £300,000 per annum. Only two areas were able to break down costs to show the average per offender attending. This reflected a more general absence of information about the numbers of offenders referred, the numbers attending at any one time, who completed and complied.

The inability of services to identify the costs of their programmes is being addressed by the Home Office, the Association of Chief Officers of Probation and Probation Committees, but a solution may be some way off.

The Prison Service is able to identify the total costs per annum and the costs per prisoner of both their sex offender programme and the two cognitive skills programmes they run. These are as follows:

Table 8.1 Cost of selected Prison Service programmes

	Cost per prisoner (approx.)	Total cost per annum
Cognitive skills		
ETS & R and R	£1,100 – £1,700	£1.92 – £2.97m
SOTP		
Core programme	£3,300	£1.96m
Booster	£1,400	£0.2m
Extended	£3,300	£0.17m
Central costs		£1.0m
TOTAL		**£5.25 - 6.29m**

During 1997 around 2,500 prisoners will have completed one or other of the above programmes, at an average cost of £2,000–£2,500. The programme costs are calculated on the basis of actual staff time involved in their delivery. Central costs include training, quality control/audit and evaluation. Given that the approximate average annual cost of keeping an inmate in prison is £24,000 (£37,000 if capital costs are included) the amount spent on the above programmes (roughly 6% of the total annual cost of a prison place) is relatively small.

If these programmes can achieve the reductions in reconvictions (and hence in further custodial sentences) which the research suggests are realistic, they should at the very least be cost neutral to the Prison Service. However, these gains will not be achieved for all prisoners. In particular, it takes some time for prison regimes to impinge greatly on an offender's future lifestyle and around two-thirds of sentenced prisoners discharged in any year have served less than six months since they were sentenced.

A full cost benefit analysis would, of course, include other financial savings and social benefits which would accrue if even a small proportion of offenders who complete such programmes cease to reoffend. Such questions cannot be answered on the basis of existing information and the Prison Service is taking steps to improve its measurement of regime effectiveness.

Conclusions

There is a broad consensus in the research literature that certain types of intervention with offenders can be effective in reducing future offending. The largest reductions are reported in the case of community-based programmes but where programmes are constructed and delivered in accordance with principles of 'what works' drawn from research, positive results have been reported following release from custody. There have, however, been very few well-designed and carefully evaluated studies in this country of the effectiveness of programmes designed to rehabilitate and reduce the risk of reoffending. Both the Prison and Probation Services are under increasing pressure to demonstrate that the programmes they run for offenders adopt the methods which research has shown are likely to be most effective and are targeted on offenders most at risk.

Systems of accreditation, which both services are developing for programmes designed to tackle offending behaviour, should ensure greater consistency of practice, a higher overall standard of work with offenders and improvements in the information available about those who attend and complete programmes. Closer collaboration between the two services is essential to ensure that work carried out in prison to reduce risk and address treatment needs is built upon during the period of post-release supervision through compatible offending behaviour programmes.

There is considerable scope for evaluative studies in this country which will provide an understanding of the types of intervention which work best with different types of offenders. More also needs to be known about the optimum level of intervention for different levels of risk (questions concerning duration and intensity of work) and the further work needed to reinforce what has been learnt in the course of a programme in order to sustain long-term reductions in offending. Finally, improvements to the collection of data by the Prison and Probation Services on programme costs will provide a better basis for examining relative cost-effectiveness.

References

Andrews, D.A., (1995) The psychology of criminal conduct and effective treatment. In (J. McGuire (Ed.) *"What Works?: Reducing Reoffending".* Chichester: Wiley.

Andrews et.al., (1990) Does correctional treatment work? A clinically relevant and psychologically informed meta-analysis. *Criminology,* 28, 369-404.

Andrews, D.A., and Bonta, J., (1994) *The Psychology of Criminal Conduct,* Cincinnati: Anderson.

Burnett, R., (1996) *Fitting Supervision to Offenders: assessment and allocation decisions in the Probation Service.* Home Office Research Study 153. London: Home Office.

Beckett, R., Beech. A., Fisher, D., and Fordham, A.S., (1994). *Community-based treatment for sex offenders: an evaluation of seven treatment programmes.* Occasional Paper. London: Home Office.

Borduin, C.M., Mann, B.J., Cone, L.T., Henggeler, S.W., Fucci, B.R., Blaske, D.M., and Williams, R.A., (1995) "Multisystematic Treatment and Serious Juvenile Offenders: Long-Term Prevention of Criminality and Violence: *Journal of Consulting and Clinical Psychology:* Vol. 63. No. 4 pp 569-578.

Copas, J., and P. Marshall (1998) The Offender Group Reconviction Scale: a statistical reconviction score for use by Probation Officers. *Applied Statistics,* 47, 159-171.

Crow, I., P. Richardson, C. Riddington and F. Simon (1989). *Unemployed, Crime and Offenders.* London: Routledge.

Ditchfield, J., (1989). *Offending on Parole.* In Home Office Research Bulletin No. 26. London: Home Office.

Edmunds, M., May, T., Hearnden, I., and Hough, M., (1997) *Drug Interventions and Prevention in the Criminal Justice System.* Unpublished paper.

Farrington, D.P., (1995) *The Development of Offending and Anti-social Behaviour from Children.* Key findings from the Cambridge Study in Delinquent Development: Journal of Child Psychology and Psychiatry, Vol. 36.

Flannagan, T., (1982) Risk and timing of recidivism in three cohorts in prison releases. *Criminal Justice Review,* 7: 32-45.

Grubin, D., and Thornton, D., (1994). A National Program for the Assessment and Treatment of Sex Offenders in the English Prison System. *Criminal Justice and Behaviour,* 21, pp 55-71.

Hann, G.H., and others (1991) Does parole reduce the risk of reconviction? *The Howard Journal,* Vol 30. No.1.

Hedderman, C., and Sugg, D., (1996)*"Does Treating Sex Offenders Reduce Reoffending?"* Research Finding No. 45. London: Home Office

Hedderman, C., and Sugg, D., (1997) Part II, *The influence of cognitive approaches: a survey of probation programmes.* Changing offenders attitudes and behaviour: What Works? HORS 171. London: Home Office

Hollin C. R., and E J. Palmer (1995) *Assessing Prison Regimes. a review to inform the development of outcome measures.* Report for the Prison Service. Birmingham: University of Birmingham (unpublished).

Home Office (1995) *"Managing What Works"* Unpublished Conference Report May 1995.

Hough, M., (1996) *Drugs Misuse and the Criminal Justice System: a review of the literature.* CDPU Paper No. 15. London: Home Office.

Lipsey, M.W., (1992)."The effect of treatment on juvenile delinquents: results from mea-analysis". In: Losel, E, Bliesener, T. and Bender, D. (Eds) *Psychology and Law: International Perspectives,* Berlin: de Gruyter.

Lloyd, C., Mair, G., and Hough, M., (1994). *Explaining reconviction rates: a critical analysis.* Home Office Research Study No. 136. London: HMSO

Lösel, F., (1995) Increasing Consensus in the Evaluation of Offender Rehabilitation? Lessons from recent research syntheses. *Psychology, Crime and Law,* Vol 2, pp 19-39.

MacKenzie, D.L., Brame, R., McDowall, D., and Souryal, C., (1995) Boot camp prisons and recidivism in eight states. *Criminology, 33,* 327-357.

Maguire, M., Peroud, B., and Raynor. P., (1996). *Automatic Conditional Release: the first two years.* Home Office Research Study No. 156. London: Home Office.

Mair, G., and May, C., (1997) *Offenders on Probation.* Home Office Research Study No. 167. London: Home Office

Marshall, P., (1995). *A statistical study of parole and reconvictions.* Unpublished note by the Home Office, London.

McGuire, J., (1996) *"Cognitive-Behavioural Approaches: An Introductory Course on Theory and Research".* Course Manual: University of Liverpool.

McMurran, M., (1996) "Alcohol, Drugs and Criminal Behaviour" In: Hollin, C (Ed) *Working with Offenders: Psychological Practices in Offender Rehabilitation.* Chichester, Wiley.

Motiuk, L. (1997). The Community Risk/Needs Management Scale: an effective supervision tool. *Forum*, Vol. 9 No. 1: Correctional Service, Canada.

Nuttall, C.P., et. al. (1977). *Parole in England and Wales.* Home Office Research Study No. 38: London: HMSO.

Player, E., and Martin C., (1996) *The ADT Drug Treatment Programme at HMP Downview - A Preliminary Evaluation.* Home Office Research Findings No. 31: Home Office, London

Porporino, F.J., and Robinson D., (1992) *Can Educating Adult Offenders Counteract Recidivism?* Correctional Service of Canada, Research Report 22.

Raynor, P., and Vanstone, M., (1996) Reasoning and Rehabilitation in Britain: The Results of the Straight Thinking on Probation (STOP) Programme. *International Journal of Offending Therapy and Comparative Criminology*, 40(4), pp 272-284: Sage.

Roberts, K., Barton. A., Buchanan, J. and Goldson, B., (1996). *Evaluation of a Home Office Initiative to Help Offenders into Employment.* Dept of Sociology, Social Policy and Social Work Studies, University of Liverpool: London, Home Office

Robinson, D., (1995). *The Impact of Cognitive Skills Training on Post-release Recidivism among Canadian Federal Offenders.* Correctional Service of Canada Research Report.

Ross, R.R., Fabiano, E., and Diemer-Ewles, C., (1988). Reasoning and Rehabilitation. *International Journal of Offender Therapy and Comparative Criminology*, 32.

Raynor, P., (1997) *Evaluating Probation: a moving target.* In G. Mair (Ed.) Evaluating the Effectiveness of Community Penalties. Avebury.

Simon, F., and C. Corbett (1996). *An Evaluation of Prison Work and Training.* Occasional Paper. London: Home Office.

Thornton, D., (1991). Treatment of Sexual Offenders in Prison: In *A strategy: treatment programmes for sex offenders in custody.* London: Home Office Directorate of Inmate Programmes, HM Prison Service.

Vennard, J., Sugg, D., and Hedderman, C., (1997) *"The use of cognitive-behavioural approaches with offenders: messages from the research".* Part I. Home Office Research Study No. 171. London: Home Office.

Ward, D., (1987). *The Validity of Reconviction Prediction Score.* Home Office Research Study No. 94: London: HMSO

Section IV
Conclusions

9 Comparative effectiveness of different approaches

Peter Goldblatt

The purpose of this report was to identify from the available research evidence interventions that are likely to be effective in reducing crime. Where possible, by comparing cost-effectiveness, strength of evidence, risk and timescales, we provide a basis for identifying options to take forward a package of interventions likely to have the most cost-effective impact on crime. To this end, the evidence presented in previous sections on each of these issues is summarised and compared in this chapter. Where gaps in our knowledge limit the comparisons that can be made, these are identified.

Key findings

Reducing criminality

There is evidence that a wide range of initiatives will prevent criminality or reduce related risk factors if they target:

- children;

- families and friends; and,

- schools.

Some of these initiatives appear to be cost-effective, with the best producing substantial returns on an initial investment. Many programmes have also been shown not to work. These tend to be based on single measure interventions.

The risk factors for later criminal behaviour include: poverty and poor housing; poor parenting (including neglect, abuse, harsh and inconsistent discipline, lack of supervision and marital conflict); association with delinquent peers, siblings and partners; low measures of intelligence, poor school performance and persistent truancy; high levels of impulsiveness and hyperactivity; and being brought up by a criminal parent or parents.

Although we cannot predict accurately which individual will become an offender on the basis of the risks to which they are exposed, we do know that children exposed to multiple risks and those who engage in anti-social or criminal behaviour at an early age are more likely to end up as serious or persistent offenders.

These risk factors are generally part of a pattern of childhood anti-social behaviour and differ little from risk factors associated with other youthful deviant behaviour. Thus, programmes to prevent criminality can be part of wider programmes to address a range of problematic outcomes for young people, such as substance abuse, school failure and teenage pregnancy. In theory at least, such programmes can be highly cost-effective since the return on any given investment will extend well beyond reductions in criminality.

This suggests that, to be effective, prevention programmes should target risk factors affecting all the main aspects of a child's life. Early interventions to target not only the children at risk but also their parents and their schools are most beneficial. They deliver multiple outcomes, are generally more cost-effective than initiatives whose focus is only to prevent crime and reductions in some of the relevant risk factors are observable within a relatively short duration.

However, most of the evidence is based on studies from North America. We cannot be sure that what works in one country will work equally well in another. The widespread ownership of firearms, the absence of a public health service, the ethnic minority composition of many inner city areas and the widespread use of drugs are just some of the features of American society which are different from ours. It is important therefore that we develop strategies for testing preventive interventions in England and Wales.

There are many promising approaches in England and Wales which have yet to be rigorously evaluated. Issues of targeting, such as the universal allocation of resources versus focusing on neighbourhoods or families, also need to be addressed, to ensure cost-effective implementation is possible. One approach would be to develop an initiative in a selection of appropriate small areas, concentrating resources in existing institutions, such as family centres and schools. This would provide a constructive intermediate stage between moving from project-based interventions on a small scale to the mainstreaming of policies to prevent criminality and related outcomes on a national scale.

Situational crime prevention: local initiatives

Situational prevention aims to act on the immediate precursors of criminal events, by influencing the offender's decision or ability to commit crimes at particular places and times, rather than by affecting offenders' propensities or motives or the local conditions which enhance these. There is a considerable body of evidence on the strengths of situational prevention:

- it can strengthen and build upon self-protection instincts;

- interventions are highly focused – facilitating finely-tuned prevention and cost effective targeting (e.g. repeat victimisation, hot spots, hot products). Focusing is based on well-developed principles, with relatively low risk of 'drift of objectives' and directly quantifiable performance indicators;

- intractable social problems are by-passed, as is the need for confrontation with police and subsequent criminalisation;

- it protects targets, rather than relying on treatment or incapacitation of offenders. This is particularly useful where catching or convicting offenders is difficult or where replacement of those caught is common;

- removing temptation from less serious crime can have a 'multiplier' effect if it prevents entry to a criminal career; and,

- the short time to implement and impact can provide 'quick wins' which can be demonstrated to deliver rapid returns on investment, facilitate fine tuning and deal promptly with emerging crime problems.

Evaluations in situational prevention are particularly well-developed and indicate potential pitfalls during implementation:

- propensity or motives for offending are not addressed;

- there may be displacement of offending to other, less-well protected targets, times and places (although research indicates this is generally of small magnitude and may be offset by diffusion of benefits);

- few universal remedies exist – what works is often heavily context-dependent;

- for many local crime problems, implementation has to be piecemeal and requires expert tailoring to individual situations; and,

- some of the most effective solutions require '*action at a distance*' -where those locally or nationally responsible for reducing crime have to get others to be more vigilant, use security, or incorporate security in their design specifications (described in more detail below).

In general, one of the most serious knowledge gaps in situational prevention is how long the effects last. Many currently effective methods grow obsolete as offenders circumvent them, realise the risk is illusory (e.g. CCTV linked to inadequate responses) or develop countermeasures. Social and technological change brings new targets (laptop computers), new tools (cordless drills) and new ways of disseminating criminal techniques (Internet). A continual programme of new initiatives is needed to maintain deterrence. If we do not monitor new and emerging opportunities for crime and take steps to keep up (see below), crime will quickly grow.

Changing the context of crime

If we are to reduce the opportunities for crime, the report indicates that it is necessary to change the way government, manufacturers and the public think and behave. Many means of crime control are already to hand. It is the motive to deploy them which is lacking. New structures are needed to increase incentives for crime prevention, particularly for dealing with innovation. These might include giving greater emphasis to identifying emerging crime patterns and opportunities and to influence others to pay more attention to crime control ramifications of technological and social change. In particular:

- there should be a review of incentives and sanctions on businesses and other institutions that generate opportunities for crime, so as to create self-interest in crime reduction (e.g. through national and local taxation);

- greater emphasis could be given to the effect of soft incentives and sanctions on action, for example, routine collection and dissemination of data to highlight differences in the rates of product crime experienced by organisations (e.g. bank robberies, credit card frauds, car thefts);

- where there is innovation crime consequences should be anticipated and counter-moves incorporated in designs (e.g. digital TV). This could be encouraged through bodies involved in design, by putting further resources into "attack testing" and by incentives to foster specialist security services; and,

- more consideration could be given to, and research undertaken on, future environments for crime, such as the Internet.

Community crime prevention

Community crime prevention – actions intended to change the social conditions which sustain crime in residential communities – focuses on the ability of local social institutions to reduce crime. The chief justification for community-based crime prevention is that high rates of crime are a feature of certain residential communities. The rationale for community prevention can stem from either a belief that common, causal reasons for crime and other social problems can be found in the social and material conditions of such communities, or that it is more efficient to target preventive measures in places which display multiple problems.

The community distribution of crime risk is very unequal. Over a half of all property crimes recorded in surveys, and over a third of all property crime victims, are likely to be found in just a fifth of the communities in England and Wales. One of the distinctive features of the growth of crime and other problems in these communities are concentration effects – the ways in which social difficulties can ratchet together and amplify each other into a spiral of deterioration. Various kinds of concentration effect seem to occur in high crime communities in Britain, including:

- young people deeply embedded in a criminal way of life;

- high levels of environmental disorder (including vandalism and graffiti);

- localised repeat victimisation;

- diminishing informal control; and,

- criminal networks on high-crime estates.

There now seems to be a consensus internationally that community crime prevention is best delivered through inter-agency co-ordination at the local level. Nevertheless, structures and arrangements vary in different ways from country to country. Where difficulties and problems of implementation have been encountered in Britain, their origins can be found in part in the structures and processes of local governance, including:

- endemic difficulties in providing co-ordinated services to specific targeted groups ;

- relations between criminal justice and local authority agencies;

- 'quasi-market' regimes for managing performance and efficiency, which make co-ordinated crime prevention a 'costly' option for local agencies; and,

- difficulties of co-ordination and implementation can lead to waste, inefficiency and lack of effectiveness in the local delivery of crime prevention.

The provisions of the forthcoming Crime and Disorder Bill will change some of these circumstances as there will be statutory clarification of some of these responsibilities and duties and a mechanism for developing an overarching framework for local action.

Most community-based programmes often resemble 'comprehensive community initiatives' (CCIs) – programmes consisting of a mixture of measures and implementation strategies which aim to bring about change holistically in local areas. However, there are major methodological and practical difficulties in evaluating the effectiveness of these and very few crime prevention CCIs have been evaluated with any great degree of scientific rigour.

While it is possible to assemble relevant evidence and promising examples of good practice – which may be regarded as an adequate basis for policy making – clear, general and scientifically reliable statements about 'what works' in community crime prevention cannot yet be made. The research evidence so far assembled does however support the strategic importance of targeting crime prevention efforts on high crime communities and applying comprehensive community initiatives to tackle the interlocking problems of social dislocation, of which crime plays an important part.

Effective policing

Policing is central to much crime prevention activity, as well as being the first port of call in dealing with offenders. It is also very complex and any discussion of improving police effectiveness or obtaining better value for money must focus on the trade-offs between different styles and methods of policing. Simply abandoning apparently ineffective methods is likely to have unforeseen consequences.

There are broadly two research approaches to effectiveness, the first – used more in the US – can be summarised as randomised allocation of some strategy to a range of areas; the second, as in-depth study of a strategy in a small number of areas has been favoured more in the UK. The former will show in broad terms *whether* something works; the latter offers some hope of understanding *how* and *why* an intervention works and of tuning it to exert maximum effect in whatever practical circumstances it is applied.

A number of strategies do not seem to be effective in terms of reducing crime, although they often have other purposes as well:

- random patrols do not have a marked effect upon crime levels;

- increasing the arrest rate through higher charging rates per crime does not have any noticeable effect on crime levels; and,

- juveniles arrested and charged for minor offences are more likely to re-offend, particularly where processing is highly 'legalistic'.

Maintenance of good community relations is clearly important but the attempts by the police to become closer to the public and involve them in addressing policing problems have been shown to be less successful than others (e.g. Neighbourhood Watch, which is predominately active in low crime areas, and solely increasing the quantity and quality of police-citizen contacts). Disrupting business in areas and houses where drug dealing takes place does not seem to reduce other crimes and the best mix of tactics against drug markets will vary according to local circumstances.

The evidence shows that some practices are effective, including:

- targeting high profile, repeat offenders with the aim of securing sound evidence, convictions and long sentences;

- targeting repeat victims, to reduce the incidence of further victimisation and as a result significantly reduce overall crime levels;

- police patrols, directed at places and times where crime is known to occur ('hot-spots'); and,

- targeting drink driving.

Some approaches are showing considerable promise:

- community participation in priority setting so as to involve citizens in high crime areas in a way that Neighbourhood Watch fails to do;

- effort put into reducing fear and suspicion of the police, and treating people (including offenders) with respect has (a) a positive effect on the degree of co-operation the police get from the community; (b) it lowers the *'perceived* serious crime level' and (c) it reduces recidivism for domestic violence;

- specific domestic violence strategies (such as the arrest of suspects) appear to work in some contexts but not others; and,

- concentrating police effort on a small area with particular crime problems and policing it very strictly (order maintenance) can reduce serious crime in the short term, but there are question marks over the long term (the consequences of arresting many more people for relatively minor offences and the poor police-community relations that follow some implementations).

None of the strategies/tactics which are proven to succeed seem to have much potential to reduce overall crime levels in isolation. A common feature of several (e.g. directed patrol and targeting repeat offenders) is that they stem from problem analysis – considering the information about a specific issue and its community context, devising solutions and then developing mechanisms for implementation. Proponents of problem oriented policing (POP) suggest that policing should be about solving underlying problems in the community which come to the attention of the police. To do this, a service must be oriented to creating the conditions and providing the resources to allow problem solving to take place routinely. This is more a style of policing than a single strategy or tactic. It appears that styles such as this - which develop improvements in the capacity of police to capture relevant data and put it to effective use, in their management techniques and in their willingness to adopt good practice - are likely to provide the best framework for increasing police effectiveness in reducing crime.

Sentencing policy

Where an offender is caught, there is evidence that early interventions are effective. Evidence from successive reconviction studies indicates that cautions administered by the police are associated with low reconviction rates if confined to first offenders. This is now included in guidance on their use. Caution plus, a formal caution with additional requirements, is a more recent innovation. So far as their impact has been measured, caution plus schemes appear to have lower reconviction rates than other formal interventions with young offenders, although no rigorous comparisons are available – follow-up has so far been limited and the trials selective.

Restorative justice, another recent innovation, seeks to provide reparation to the victim, and to make the offender take responsibility for his or her actions. The aim is to restore the well-being of victims and of the community damaged by crime and to prevent reoffending. In some schemes the offender is diverted from formal proceedings, although it can be part of a court disposal or caution plus. Initial indications from evaluations are that both victims and offenders consider them to be procedurally fair and victims tend to be more satisfied. Reconviction rates of the caution plus schemes with a restorative element are low, but have yet to be formally evaluated.

Sentencing by courts is used to fulfil a variety of purposes simultaneously:

- deterrence;

- incapacitation;

- rehabilitation;

- fairness and equity;

- retribution; and,

- maintaining confidence in the CJS.

On occasions one of these objectives will predominate. More often sentencers seek to balance different objectives. Reconviction studies over the years have told a consistent story: any apparent differences between sentences, in terms of their impact on reoffending rates, are largely the result of other factors, such as the age and criminal history of the offender. There is also increasing evidence of a link between drug usage and other forms of crime. Criminal punishment does have a deterrent effect, although it is not clear how much extra deterrence can be achieved by increasing the severity of punishment. For this to happen, potential offenders need to be aware that the risks have changed and it appears that this is often not the case.

Custody is the most expensive disposal, and is no more successful at preventing offenders obtaining further convictions than other disposals. But it protects the public from the risk of further harm from the offender while the imprisonment lasts, and satisfies the public need for retribution in respect of serious offenders. Various estimates have been made of the overall impact of imprisonment on levels of crime. In 1994, based on levels of imprisonment and crime prevailing at that time, it was estimated that a 25 per cent increase in the prison population of England and Wales was needed to achieve a one per cent fall in crime.

In comparing non-custodial disposals, likely consequences on future behaviour is the primary concern. There is evidence that curfew orders with tagging are viewed as a severe non-custodial penalty and are being imposed as a genuine alternative to custody and higher end community penalties in some pilot areas in England and Wales. Community service (CS) can achieve rehabilitative goals with some offenders, if focused on practising positive social behaviour and new skills.

There are probation programmes which can have an impact on offending (see below), but these tend to require more resources than straight probation (which does not appear to have much effect on offending). The resources of the Probation Service should therefore not be dissipated on those for whom a fine would serve as well. To do so may have the perverse effect of diluting the impact that the Probation Service can have on those for whom intensive intervention would bear fruit. It would also result in moving less serious offenders up the "tariff stepladder", resulting in a greater chance of progression to subsequent imprisonment. Reconviction rates for fines compare favourably with community penalties. Although this largely reflects their selective use, there is no evidence that the switch from fines to community penalties that has occurred over the past 20 years has achieved anything by way of crime reduction.

Interventions with offenders and drug users

There is a broad consensus from research that certain types of intervention with offenders in custody and in the community can be effective in reducing future offending. The largest reported reductions are from community-based programmes constructed and delivered in accordance with principles of 'what works' drawn from research. Positive results have also been reported for custody-based programmes that follow these principles.

The most effective programmes for addressing offending behaviour are designed to:

* be skills-based;

* improve problem-solving; and,

* draw on behavioural techniques to reinforce improved conduct.

There are consistent indications that cognitive behavioural approaches are more successful than techniques such as unfocused group or individual counselling and unstructured therapy. Typically:

* cognitive-behavioural programmes achieve around a 15 percentage point lower reconviction rate when delivered non-selectively to a broad range of offenders than that reported for similar offenders who did not attend such programmes;

* larger reductions in recidivism (around 20 percentage points lower than control groups) have been reported for programmes which follow the effectiveness principles closely, and,

- programmes which also include training in social skills show the most positive results with both juvenile and adult offenders.

Although probation services in England and Wales frequently incorporate cognitive-behavioural or cognitive skills approaches in their work with offenders, the evidence suggests that programme integrity is poor and staff training inadequate. Despite evidence that focused and targeted programmes are more effective, general programmes were more popular and there is little sign that offenders are selected appropriately.

Some types of programmes and placements show particular promise. Early indications are that sex-offender programmes can produce positive early results. Vocational training, literacy provision and employment related projects can reduce reconviction rates. Drug misuse treatment programmes in the community can be successful, if started quickly (and hence used in conjunction with early identification and immediate access to treatment), continued for as long as possible and carried out in a positive and supportive environments. Research has identified "vulnerable" groups with higher than average risk of developing addictive or dependent drug use (including the young homeless, truants, those excluded from school, young offenders and young people looked after by local authorities). Prevention programmes targeted at these groups are likely to be more successful than more general ones.

There have been very few well-designed and carefully evaluated studies in this country of the effectiveness of programmes designed to rehabilitate and reduce the risk of reoffending. Both the Prison and Probation Services are under increasing pressure to demonstrate that the programmes they run for offenders adopt the methods which research shows are likely to be most effective and are targeted on offenders most at risk.

Systems of accreditation, which both services are developing for programmes designed to tackle offending behaviour, should ensure greater consistency of practice, a higher overall standard of work with offenders and improvements in the information available about those who attend and complete programmes. Closer collaboration between the two services is essential to ensure that work carried out in prison to reduce risk and address treatment needs is built upon during the period of post-release supervision through compatible offending behaviour programmes.

Comparisons of effectiveness and cost-effectiveness

The evidence for effectiveness

The evidence summarised in this report points to a range of interventions for which there is evidence, or the promise of, effectiveness in reducing crime. Much of the more thoroughly evaluated evidence comes from the US and there is an open question as to whether it would be equally effective in England and Wales (or, in some cases, whether it is appropriate to conditions here). Conversely, some initiatives which are claimed to work in the UK have not been rigorously evaluated.

This suggests that we should proceed cautiously in adopting the relevant interventions, undertaking implementation on a large scale only when they have been shown to be effective on a smaller scale and once implementation strategies have been adequately tested. This points to the need for pilots of a size that is adequate for rigorous process and impact evaluation.

Many of the promising interventions deliver their main crime reduction effects over the medium or longer term. This, and the wide variety of groups and organisations needed to implement the relevant interventions, also suggest that implementation of interventions shown to be effective in small-scale pilots may not replicate their success on a larger scale if objectives are allowed to drift. Even in shorter-term initiatives (such as offender programmes), there is evidence that there is a dilution of 'what works' principles when applied on a large scale. To avoid these risks, close monitoring and evaluation must be included as integral components of an implementation programme. Regular reviews, based on this information, should help to ensure that the principles on which the programmes are based are maintained stringently enough for them to deliver reductions in crime effectively.

Cost-benefit analyses

Although it was possible to identify some information that supported cost-benefit analyses (particularly in preventing criminality and in situational prevention), there are many areas where the research conducted does not support rigorous, or even approximate, cost-benefit analysis. To ensure that interventions are only adopted on a large scale when they are shown to be effective, both cost and effectiveness information are required from process and impact evaluations.

The evaluation of Safer Cities has indicated how information on costs can be related to effectiveness in this country, providing a rational basis for deciding on the most appropriate level of investment. In this instance, reduction in burglary risk through Safer Cities action was greater where there was more intense burglary action – but to achieve these bigger falls cost disproportionately more. This can best be illustrated by contrasting two strategies for a *national* impact of Safer Cities-type burglary action:

- targeting higher-risk areas – amounting to a tenth of the country's 20 million households – gives a 5.5 per cent reduction in national burglary rates (and a hence 0.6 per cent reduction in overall recorded crime). The return on this is *one-and-a-half times more than the spend* (£95 million gross return on £38 million spend); or,

- covering half the country's households reduces the national burglary rate by 12 per cent but savings are only *a third more than the spend* (£204 million gross return on £151 million spend).

For comparison, the evidence suggests that the cost of achieving a reduction of around 0.6 per cent in crime through increases in the prison population alone would be about £380 million a year.

Conclusions

Taken together, the evidence in this report provides the basis for a coherent and co-ordinated strategy which recognises that:

- none of the initiatives identified as promising will control crime on its own. An effective crime reduction strategy is one in which an integrated package of best practice is developed and delivered consistently over time;

- multiple interventions are generally more cost-effective than initiatives with a single focus. For example, prevention programmes for young people should target risk factors affecting all aspects of a child's life;

- advantage should be taken of evidence which identifies particular initiatives which would have an early but not necessarily lasting effect on offending behaviour and therefore the crime rate;

- many promising initiatives bring their main crime reduction benefits over a long period. However they have earlier, beneficial effects on other outcomes (education, employment, informal social control and family cohesion), the absence of which are predictors of subsequent criminality. The effect on these risk factors therefore needs to be carefully monitored, evaluated and reviewed to ensure the full potential of the initiatives is realised (and ineffectual interventions stopped);

- implementation of initiatives more generally should be planned so as to ensure that the 'what works' principles are adhered to and adequate and appropriate training and evaluation are included. The evidence that emerges from evaluation should be used to inform the running and performance monitoring of the main Government programmes to which they relate; and,

- evidence on effectiveness, and more particularly cost effectiveness, is currently limited, cannot easily be extrapolated nationally from small-scale pilots and is not collected in a way which allows for comparisons between initiatives. Process and impact evaluation should therefore be designed to generate both cost and effectiveness information.

The findings summarised in this chapter suggest that an integrated strategy would be effective if it included:

- intensive interventions among children and families at risk;

- increasing informal social control and social cohesion in communities and institutions that are vulnerable to crime, criminality, drug usage and disorder;

- intervention in the development of products or services vulnerable to crime so as to make them less so;

- incentives to individuals and organisations to reduce the risk of crime;

- targeting situational prevention measures on "hot spots" and areas of high risk generally;

- reducing repeat victimisation;

- placing greater emphasis on problem oriented policing;

- extending the range of effective interventions with offenders and drug users;

- making more use, in appropriate circumstances, of penalties such as fines and curfew orders with tagging; and,

- improving the consistency of sentencing.

Such a portfolio would combine long term investment in children and families with actions that would yield more immediate, though probably smaller returns (such as situational prevention). It would also include activities aimed at achieving gains that accumulate steadily (such as offender programmes, community action and improved product design). Implementation on a large scale would be undertaken only when promising initiatives had been shown to be effective on a small scale and implementation strategies adequately tested There is evidence that such an approach would be cost effective throughout its life, with substantial cost benefits in the long run.

Annex A
Assessing the strength of research evidence

Sherman et al., 1997, conducted a review of the scientific literature, to inform an evaluation of the effectiveness of the US Department of Justice's grants to assist in the prevention of crime (see Chapter 1). They employed a scientific methods scale to rate the 'methodological rigor' of the studies quoted in evidence. The five levels identified by this scale are used descriptively in several chapters of this report (although they have not formed the sole basis for judging effectiveness or strength of evidence). The method used by Sherman et al. (1997) for assigning a score to a study is described below.

Scientific methods scale

Studies examined by Sherman et al. (1997) were given an overall rating (from 1 to 5). They used several different dimensions but primarily based the score on these factors:

- the study's ability to control extraneous variables;

- the minimization of measurement error: and,

- the statistical power to detect meaningful differences.

The core criteria required to achieve the five levels of scientific rigour were:

1) correlation between a crime prevention programme and a measure of crime or crime risk factors;

2) temporal sequence between the programme and the crime or risk outcome clearly observed, or a comparison group present without demonstrated comparability to the treatment group;

3) a comparison between two or more units of analysis, one with and one without the programme;

4) comparison between multiple units within and without the programme, controlling for other factors, or a non-equivalent comparison group has only minor differences evident; or,

5) random assignment and analysis of comparable units to programme and comparison groups.

Deciding what works

In terms of this five-level scale, Sherman et al., 1997, found that scores for most of the available evaluations were low. They did not meet the high threshold for rigour set by the authors for recommending what works. Based on the scientific strength and substantive findings of the available evidence, their report therefore classifies programmes into four categories:

What works

Programmes that are reasonably likely to be effective in the kinds of contexts in which they were evaluated and for which the findings should be generalisable to similar settings in other places and times. These must have at least two level 3 evaluations with statistical significance tests showing effectiveness and the preponderance of all available evidence supporting the same conclusion.

What's promising

These are programmes for which the level of certainty from available evidence is too low to support generalisable conclusions but for which there is some empirical evidence for predicting that further research could support such conclusions. Programmes are regarded as promising if they have at least one level 3 evaluation with significance tests showing effectiveness and the preponderance of all available evidence supporting the same conclusion.

What doesn't work

Programmes that we are reasonably certain fail to be effective in the kinds of contexts in which they were evaluated and for which the findings should be generalisable to similar settings in other places and times. These must have at least two level 3 evaluations with statistical significance tests showing ineffectiveness and the preponderance of all available evidence supporting the same conclusion.

What's unknown

Any programme not falling into one of the other three categories.

Publications

List of research publications

The most recent research reports published are listed below. A **full** list of publications is available on request from the Research and Statistics Directorate Information and Publications Group.

Home Office Research Studies (HORS)

173. **Ethnic monitoring in police forces: a beginning.** Marian FitzGerald and Rae Sibbitt. 1997.

174. **In police custody: Police powers and suspects' rights under the revised PACE codes of practice.** Tom Bucke and David Brown. 1997.

176. **The perpetrators of racial harassment and racial violence.** Rae Sibbitt. 1997.

177. **Electronic monitoring in practice: the second year of the trials of curfew orders.** Ed Mortimer and Chris May. 1997.

178. **Handling stolen goods and theft: A market reduction approach.** Mike Sutton. 1998.

179. **Attitudes to punishment: findings from the British Crime Survey.** Michael Hough and Julian Roberts. 1998.

180. **Sentencing Practice: an examination of decisions in magistrates' courts and the Crown Court in the mid–1990's.** Claire Flood-Page and Alan Mackie. 1998.

181. **Coroner service survey.** Roger Tarling. 1998.

182. **The prevention of plastic and cheque fraud revisited.** Michael Levi and Jim Handley. 1998.

183. **Drugs and crime: the results of research on drug testing and interviewing arrestees.** Trevor Bennett. 1998.

Research Findings

52. **Police cautioning in the 1990s.** Roger Evans and Rachel Ellis. 1997.

53. **A reconviction study of HMP Grendon Therapeutic Community.** Peter Marshall. 1997.

54. **Control in category c prisons.** Simon Marshall. 1997.

55. **The prevalence of convictions for sexual offending.** Peter Marshall. 1997.

56. **Drug misuse declared in 1996: key results from the British Crime Survey.** Malcolm Ramsay and Josephine Spiller. 1997.

57. **The 1996 International Crime Victimisation Survey.** Pat Mayhew and Phillip White. 1997.

58. **The sentencing of women: a section 95 publication.** Carol Hedderman and Lizanne Dowds. 1997.

59. **Ethnicity and contacts with the police: latest findings from the British Crime Survey.** Tom Bucke. 1997.

60. **Policing and the public: findings from the 1996 British Crime Survey.** Catriona Mirrlees-Black and Tracy Budd. 1997.

61. **Changing offenders' attitudes and behaviour: what works?** Julie Vennard, Carol Hedderman and Darren Sugg. 1997.

62. **Suspects in police custody and the revised PACE codes of practice.** Tom Bucke and David Brown. 1997.

63. **Neighbourhood watch co-ordinators.** Elizabeth Turner and Banos Alexandrou. 1997.

64. **Attitudes to punishment: findings from the 1996 British Crime Survey.** Michael Hough and Julian Roberts. 1998.

65. **The effects of video violence on young offenders.** Kevin Browne and Amanda Pennell. 1998.

66. **Electronic monitoring of curfew orders: the second year of the trials.** Ed Mortimer and Chris May. 1998.

67. **Public perceptions of drug-related crime in 1997.** Nigel Charles. 1998.

68. **Witness care in magistrates' courts and the youth court.** Joyce Plotnikoff and Richard Woolfson. 1998.

69. **Handling stolen goods and theft: a market reduction approach.** Mike Sutton. 1998.

70. **Drug testing arrestees.** Trevor Bennett. 1998.

71. **Prevention of plastic card fraud.** Michael Levi and Jim Handley. 1998.

72. **Offending on bail and police use of conditional bail.** David Brown. 1998.

73. **Voluntary after-care.** Mike Maguire, Peter Raynor, Maurice Vanstone and Jocelyn Kynch. 1998.

74. **Fast-tracking of persistent young offenders.** John Graham. 1998.

75. **Mandatory drug testing in prisons – an evaluation.** Kimmett Edgar and Ian O'Donnell. 1998.

Occasional Papers

Evaluation of a Home Office initiative to help offenders into employment. Ken Roberts, Alana Barton, Julian Buchanan and Barry Goldson. 1997.

The impact of the national lottery on the horse-race betting levy. Simon Field and James Dunmore. 1997.

The cost of fires. A review of the information available. Donald Roy. 1997.

Monitoring and evaluation of WOLDS remand prison and comparisons with public-sector prisons, in particular HMP Woodhill. A Keith Bottomley, Adrian James, Emma Clare and Alison Liebling. 1997.

Requests for Publications

Home Office Research Studies and Research Findings can be requested from:

Research and Statistics Directorate
Information and Publications Group
Room 201, Home Office
50 Queen Anne's Gate
London SW1H 9AT
Telephone: 0171-273 2084
Fascimile: 0171-222 0211
Internet: http://www.homeoffice.gov.uk/rsd/rsdhome.htm
E-mail: rsd.ho.apollo@gtnet.gov.uk

Occasional Papers can be purchased from:
Home Office
Publications Unit
50 Queen Anne's Gate
London SW1H 9AT
Telephone: 0171-273 2302

HMSO Publications Centre

(Mail, fax and telephone orders only)
PO Box 276, London SW8 5DT
Telephone orders: 0171-873 9090
General enquiries: 0171-873 0011
(queuing system in operation for both numbers)
Fax orders: 0171-873 8200